The New Elite

The New Elite

Britain's Top Chief Executives

Walter Goldsmith and Berry Ritchie

Line drawings by Matthew Ritchie

Weidenfeld and Nicolson · London

First published in Great Britain in 1987 by
George Weidenfeld & Nicolson Limited,
91 Clapham High Street, London SW4 7TA

ISBN 0 297 78990 2

Printed and bound in Great Britain by
Butler & Tanner Ltd
Frome and London

Contents

Foreword

To have a vision in the business world is rare enough; to share and communicate one requires further qualities, but it is their realization of that vision which sets the heroes of this book apart. Our comparison of the background, style and character of ten of Britain's successful chief executives proves them, we believe, worthy of the title 'The New Elite'.

The 1979–86 period in the United Kingdom has featured one political party in power: it has been the 'Thatcher era'. However, it is not the political arena in which our gladiators have fought, although they have undoubtedly been affected by it. The new elite have figured in the complex, competitive, fast-changing, economically violent business arena, but they have performed in a new environment.

The business environment during the last seven years has been one of greater freedom with debilitating and diverting controls over pay, prices, incomes, currency exchange removed. The economic condition was for much of the period recessionary and yet the Government refused to prop up the 'lame ducks': business was free to succeed or fail without Government help. Those who triumphed were recognized and their success regarded increasingly as of material importance.

There was greater incentive for those who succeeded. The top rate of income tax was reduced from 83% to 60% of earnings. The tax treatment of stock options was made considerably more attractive, enabling key executives to share in the success of their companies in unison with shareholders. Pay was more related to performance, and high salaries achieved by senior executives in this way were accepted by shareholders and other employees alike.

The power of trade union leaders decreased as their members came to terms with the new, or rediscovered, facts of business life, recognizing that there was no alternative to competitiveness, which meant greater productivity and often fewer, but more secure, jobs. In an increasing number of companies communications improved, possibly permanently, as managements facing the challenges of recession and redundancy felt compelled to explain matters to the whole workforce. They discovered, as many of us had long known, that a well-informed, involved work-force thinks of itself as employees first and trade union members second, rather than the reverse. The result has been that great change has been effected with, in most cases, a minimum of industrial disruption and substantial improvements in productivity.

New forms of co-operation have thrived, such as quality circles, consultative committees and share ownership. Barriers have been broken down in restrictive practices, demarcation and manage-ment/employee relations. All this has happened at a time when the march of technology has accelerated dramatically and relentlessly, changing the very nature of work and the workplace. The previously dethroned customer has become king again, not just for the sales and marketing teams, but as the driving force for all employees whatever their function.

Britain is no longer regarded as the prime market or marketplace for most British companies as world markets become the targets of thriving businesses. The period of substantial oil revenues has been matched by a vast acceleration of investment overseas, helping to secure new markets and sources of continuing high revenue for Britain in the future. It has been a period of deep concerns: over the future of employment as unemployment reached record levels, about the future viability of great industries like textiles or steel, over North/South gaps in Britain and North/South gaps in world prosperity. That great social scourge and source of governmental fraud on the people – high inflation – has been largely conquered in Britain and steady economic growth is perhaps within our grasp. It has been a period of triumphs, pain, progress, decline, a period of doubt, frustration and success. Above all, it has been a period of change.

This period of change has seen the emergence of a new breed of business man from the stagnating mists of corporatism; chief execu-tives who have brought back clear leadership and shared their sense of mission with all those employed in their companies. They have been catalysts of change in a changing environment.

This brings us to an explanation of why we have written this book in the way we have. We were no more aware of the achievements of Britain's new captains of industry than many people interested in the fate of Britain's economy. Indeed, their formula for success could be said to have become the received wisdom for managing large companies in crisis. But that does not explain how the New Elite managed to get it right in the first place. When they first engaged in their individual battles for survival and recovery, they were making up their strategies and tactics as they went along, on the basis of ideas and knowledge which they had acquired through their own experience.

Thus the purpose of this book is threefold. Firstly, we have, we hope, defined the formula for success that has been evolved by the New Elite. We have not done this on any academic basis, but by example, by looking at the actions taken by ten outstanding chief executives in the course of transforming the companies they have managed during some of the most testing years that British industries have ever experienced.

Secondly, we have tried to show how this select band acquired the skills and attitudes that have enabled it to succeed in practice where so many others have failed. We have looked at their social background, their education and their business careers to discover what inspired their choice of industry in the first place and why they climbed the corporate ladder so far.

Finally, we have attempted to illustrate the personalities and characteristics that make these men so remarkable, as well as the conclusions they have reached about the future of British industry.

We do not pretend to have arrived at an objective conclusion, nor do we apologize for our point of view. We believe that the one lesson which emerges from our researches is that in the end it is the individual who matters. The proper study of mankind is man, wrote Alexander Pope nearly three hundred years ago. We couldn't agree more. We believe that the New Elite are people whom aspiring young business men and women will wish to emulate, and that the following chapters will provide some insight into why they reached the top.

Finally, we would like to thank all the people who so generously gave of their time to help us. This is as much their book as ours.

The New Elite

The idea that the fate of British industry, the jobs of millions of people and the standard of living of the whole country rests in the hands of a few exceptional businessmen may seem fanciful. It is not a concept that would be supported by many. The view of British industry that comes out of any statistical analysis of its performance over the past ten, fifteen, twenty, thirty or even a hundred years is one of inevitable decline. Books have been published to prove that Britain has been in the grip of economic malaise almost from the moment the Industrial Revolution began and even the theory that as a nation we rise at the eleventh hour to meet whatever challenge we may face has been demolished. If we are to believe some historians, the British industrial war effort was more a training ground in shirking and shoddiness than an example of everyone pulling together.

This is, of course, a nonsense. During the past forty years there has been a revolution in living standards in the United Kingdom. Most of us have lives of unparalleled affluence and opportunity. Most homes have bathrooms with running hot water. Many have central heating. Walk into most kitchens and there are washing machines, dish-washers, refrigerators, electric mixing machines and microwave ovens. Then there are all the other electronic marvels so many people are rich enough to own: televisions, telephones, video recorders, home computers and stereo systems. And how many of us go on holiday to Spain, Morocco, India or the West Indies compared to forty years ago?

To suggest that all this affluence has descended on us without anyone raising a hand in a single honest day's toil is clearly absurd. British industry has been highly successful in many areas. We have been as quick as any of our industrial competitors at developing new technologies and, in spite of our much advertised penchant for failing to capitalize on our own inventiveness, we have managed to stumble along economically somehow or other. The inward-looking view of

1

British industry as a unique disaster area is not one shared by some of the countries we envy – France, for example, Italy or Sweden. They look at us and see only our advantages, our bountiful energy resources, our international language and our temperate climate.

However, it is undoubtedly true that for the last twenty years our industries have faced increasing problems. Some of them have been the result of worldwide changes, such as growing competition from many more countries in industries like steel, shipbuilding and car manufacture. Perhaps it has always been only a matter of time before our share of these industries was bound to be eroded by other countries with poorer populations and access to much richer raw materials. But so far is far enough. It is all very well to accept the need to make room for new competitors. It is an entirely different matter to let them take over completely. In industry after industry Britain has lost first its overseas markets and then its home markets to foreign manufacturers. We have suffered serious setbacks, apparently, in almost every business in which we have been a manufacturer: textiles, engineering, television, hi-fi, computers, electronics, cars, trucks, buses, even bicycles. You name it, we have had it.

There have been several factors responsible for this collapse, among them the oil price crises, galloping inflation largely caused by the revolution in energy costs and the mismanagement of the economy by successive governments, which, between them, succeeded in dismantling trade barriers protecting UK industry without obtaining reciprocal treatment from other countries and in artificially over-valuing sterling so that British goods were too expensive to export.

To a greater or lesser extent, however, a lot of our industrial competitors faced the same problems and coped with them conspicuously better. There are people who believe that the judgment of history will deal unkindly with both Labour and Conservative politicians for not creating better conditions for British business.

The contrary school of thought argues that protectionism was the real cause of the rot. Most people who hold this opinion are talking about protection given to trade unions, which resulted in the emergence of shopfloor power. This is the other favourite whipping horse for the failure of British industry. Managers, say its riders, were deprived of the power to manage. Union power protected jobs, and British companies, especially large ones, became grossly overmanned because they were not allowed to sack unproductive workers. Nor could they introduce more efficient machinery to improve output because that, too, was vetoed by militant shop stewards.

This argument is well documented. Strikes became known as the British disease. Industrial unrest reached its apogee in the nationalized industries, like British Steel and the National Coal Board, but was rife throughout the private sector as well, though not quite as consistently as may be imagined. Many companies and some industries were much less affected than others. In some, it was because the management succeeded in convincing its employees that its policies were in their long-term interest or were inevitable, while other industries, like textiles, had such a long history of redundancies and retreat in the face of foreign competition that the workers were inured to failure.

Apportioning blame for the UK's industrial plight at the end of the 1970s is, in the end, academic. The fact remains that by the beginning of the 1980s the damage had been done. Due to a combination of the above factors, large chunks of our industrial infrastructure were plunging over the edge of the abyss. To give a specific example, between 1980 and 1984 ICI estimates that one quarter of the British companies to which it sold its products disappeared. That's right – 25% of its British customers went out of business. By any standards this is a horrific rate of failure. That it was representative of industry at large was proven by the statistics compiled by the Department of Trade and Industry and organizations like the CBI. The significance to the country as a whole became clear in the first quarter of 1983, when, for the first time in our industrial history, imports of manufactured goods exceeded exports.

It could be argued that this was the inevitable consequence of sterling reflecting oil exports, rather than manufacturing competitiveness, but the collective response has been to wring our hands. The Government has done what governments always do in times of crisis, exhorted us to do better. In turn, most of us have cheerfully or miserably, depending on our circumstances and inclination, castigated the politicians, the trades unions, the Common Market, the United States, the Japanese and each other – and done nothing. But there have been exceptions. Not all British industry has, in the event, been prepared to surrender to its fate. Faced with imminent disaster, some companies resorted to radical solutions. Others, a few, had even seen the writing on the wall and had acted to protect themselves. In the last five or six years, there have been some heroic struggles to overcome the problems pressing British companies towards bankruptcy. In every case, these desperate endeavours have been inspired and led by individuals. These are the men we call the New Elite.

History is full of examples of the hour calling forth the man. As history is written by the victors, the men who are recorded tend to be cast in the heroic mould. In reality, when the counter-historians get to work, when their immediate fame has faded, the heroes often turn out to be as human as the rest of us. But that does not alter the fact that they achieve remarkable things. We believe that this claim can be made for the small group of businessmen who have been fighting a bitter rearguard action to save a large part of British industry from extinction.

What they have done is perhaps already appreciated. How they have achieved it is also known, although maybe not so widely. One of our objectives in writing this book has been to discover if there is a common formula which the New Elite have used in their efforts to overcome the problems they faced in a variety of industries. But our main attempt has been to look at the characters and background of the men themselves. The common factor running through all the companies that we have studied is that it took determined action by an individual to change the course they were so fatally pursuing. In some cases the man seized control of his company in the face of apathy or obstruction by the board. In others, the need for action had already been accepted and the hero was consciously chosen. In every case, however, the emergence of an individual leader has been the prerequisite of change.

The members of the New Elite all believe in leadership and think of themselves as leaders. Defining a leader is a subject all of its own, but in the final analysis, the test of the leader is whether others follow him. Examples of leaders in other areas are easy to find: Margaret Thatcher, of course; Admiral Sir John Woodward, the hero of the Falklands campaign; the manager of Liverpool Football Club. Er ... perhaps finding examples is not that easy. Real leaders are rare birds. Or is it that in this country leaders are only allowed the power to act when all else has failed? The curious emergence of powerful individuals at the top of a significant number of major corporations at virtually the same moment is too much of a coincidence not to reflect a common peril.

What is also notable is that they emerged from within the system.

4

It is facile to think of them as mercenaries brought in to shoot down the troublemakers. The appointment of Ian MacGregor at British Steel and the National Coal Board, and of Sir Michael Edwardes at BL may look like examples of hired guns, but this ignores the fact that both these men were chosen on the basis of their experience of running large corporations over many years. Most of the other chairmen and chief executives who comprise the New Elite rose to the top from inside their companies.

When the crunch came, the criteria applied in the selection of individuals to take charge of the crisis were not confined to subjective assessments of character and willpower. High on the list were experience and past performance. Leaders, it appears, are not just born; they also learn to lead.

The Embodiment of Power

If there is a distinguishing mark shared by successful chief executives, it is probably their air of confidence. There is no doubt that the power to say unto one go and he goeth, meaning he'll be fired on the spot if he doesn't pull his finger out, engenders a certain superiority, a tiny touch of smugness. For people responsible for thousands of jobs and billions of pounds, they look remarkably relaxed. It is a composure born of being in charge. These are not men who panic, but men who are in control of Destiny.

With few exceptions Britain's chief executives are healthy, happy men. Women don't get to the top in industry, at least not through the management route. The men in question are a little above average height, perhaps, and obviously well-fed, but also relatively fit for their age, which is on average in the early fifties. They are sedentary, but not flabby. They don't drink at lunch if they can help it and they are careful about their diets, but not in any faddy way. Some of them take exercise, running or riding bicycles to work or playing squash, but not to the point where it takes precedence over their commitment to their companies. Nothing does that. The average chief executive is, by anybody's standards, a workaholic. He seems to have no trouble getting up in the morning and his mind clicks instantly into gear, weighing up the news and marshalling the challenges of the day ahead. The working day proper begins when the chauffeur-driven company car draws up outside, at perhaps seven o'clock or maybe a little later. It is probably a Rolls or a Jaguar. It usually has a telephone and sometimes he can't resist contacting a luckless minion while he is en route. During the rest of the journey he glances through the contents of his briefcase, filling his mind with the details he needs for the meetings awaiting his arrival, of which the first may well start of 8.15.

He arrives at his office in understated style. He greets by name the uniformed sergeant, the receptionist and most of the early birds he passes on his way to his top-floor offices. Courtesy and a good memory for names is part of the equipment of the leader. His faithful personal assistant is often there when he arrives, in spite of the early hour, a pleasant, organized, mature woman with immense influence and total loyalty, who makes straight the path of the chief and guards his approaches against unauthorized or time-wasting visitors.

The first meeting leads on to the next or to a flying visit to a plant. If it is near at hand, the chief will travel by car again, but if at any distance, by jet. Few of the New Elite believe in company planes, but they travel first class as a matter of course and by the fastest means. Flying Concorde is an economy when you are paid anything up to £17,000 a week. At the company front line, he makes a point of being seen by the employees, walking through the plant, chatting to the sales girls, studiedly egalitarian in his attitudes. Most of our chief executives are practitioners of 'management by walking about', one of the hallmarks of excellence.

Some are more hail-fellow-well-met than others. Even the most reserved, however, is remarkably free of class-consciousness. There is very little 'them and us' about their behaviour. It wins them gratifying loyalty from the workers on the shopfloor. These guys, the feeling is, are really very accessible, very ordinary; the bosses, certainly, but not a bunch of snobs.

The morning over, our average chief executive may find himself at lunch with a journalist, probably one hand-picked by his public relations aide as worth massaging. Chief executives are more relaxed with the media than many businessmen, but even so they have an uneasy relationship. On the one hand they are far from impressed by the poor grasp of facts that journalists often demonstrate and are affronted by their laziness and inaccuracy, and they never think their company gets the favourable comment it deserves. On the other hand, they are flattered by the attention they receive. They are increasingly becoming media stars and the taste of fame is very sweet. Stardom is something that has come to them quite late. Most of their working lives have been spent inside large corporations, heads down, managing. They are not like pop stars, thrust into the limelight from the beginning. Nor are they entrepreneurs, like Sir Freddie Laker or Sir Clive Sinclair, who have always attracted the bubble reputation. Nor do they come from privileged backgrounds which would, whatever the drawbacks, equip them to accept homage as their birthright.

One of the most striking aspects of our sample of chief executives is their humble origins. Only one, Sir Christopher Hogg, the chairman and chief executive of Courtaulds, went to a major public school. Most of the others attended grammar schools or were educated abroad. They have all escaped the upper-class prejudice against industry – in fact they are the living proof that it exists. They are, to a man, meritocrats and Sir Peter Walters, Chairman of BP, the biggest company of them all, is the archetypal example. He went to King Edward High School, Birmingham, which, when he was a pupil, creamed off the brightest children from the five other Birmingham grammar schools through a blatantly elitist 12-plus examination. This reflects the fact that they are all extremely intelligent. They have very fine minds. It is a comforting discovery, because it means that their achievements owe little to luck, but much to talent and, of course, hard work.

In spite of their fine brains, they are not intellectuals. In part this is due to their modest family backgrounds, but it is not because they lacked opportunity. Peter Walters was a classics scholar at school and Christopher Hogg won a first-class honours degree in English at Oxford. However, most of them have degrees or comparable qualifications in practical subjects like engineering, economics, the law or accountancy, and a significant proportion went to business school.

They are not cultural philistines. Depending on their tastes, they are regular attenders at the opera, the ballet, the Royal Festival Hall and the National Theatre. Whether they would find time to go if the company did not organize their leisure, frequently merging business with pleasure, is, however, an open question. Quizzed on their reading habits by the *Financial Times*, Sir John Harvey-Jones of ICI admitted to reading Len Deighton, while Peter Walters listed *Cruising Coastline and Beyond* and *Classic Roses*. Most of the time, however, they read for information, choosing books on countries they visit, scientific or business subjects.

Lunch over, our typical chief executive is back in discussion with his senior managers. There is a good chance it will be a planning meeting. The top management team could be hiding away in a country hotel for the weekend, going through one of its operating companies' budgets for the year. Our man sits in casual judgment, listening to the case put forward by the line managers, thrusting in the occasional sharp question, encouraging a junior but coming man to lock horns with his boss and then smoothly defusing the potential conflict. The conference ends with targets pushed a little further and the need to act on problem areas sharpened.

It is difficult to assess exactly how hard they work. Everything is arranged to make sure they waste as little of their immensely valuable and expensive time as possible. They are always briefed before they meet people and they expect their staff to be equally well prepared. Meetings, they say, are not intended to exchange information, but to arrive at decisions.

Without exception they think of themselves as strategists. Compared to most businessmen, this is a justifiable conceit, but if you imagine that their success is due to their ability to think deep, far-sighted thoughts, forget it. Their real talent is the speed with which they can assess problems and then decide on action. That is their greatest strength. That is what has lifted them above their peers and placed them in the biggest, toughest jobs in industry. They take decisions and then make them happen. 'Do it now!' says Sir Michael Edwardes. 'Let's go with it!' says Richard Giordano of BOC.

All our top chief executives are brilliant at handling meetings. They profess not to like them, but this is not true. They love them. What they hate are meetings which don't produce results. Not surprisingly they are past masters at controlling meetings so that matters proceed swiftly and directly towards the conclusion they planned in the first place.

They wouldn't put it like that. They like to think they have open minds, ready to respond to any positive ideas put forward. This is true, but they also usually have very sharply defined opinions of their own. They are open to persuasion, but it takes a very well prepared case to divert them from a course of action that they have already decided upon. And they all admit there are times when they listen to all the arguments and then do something different. Any idea that these men are democratic should be swiftly abandoned. We are writing about some of the most singleminded people in business. The most accurate description of their real nature might be beneficent dictators, a form of rule described by somebody, probably Machiavelli, as the best there is.

It is, however, true that they win the wholehearted support of their senior colleagues, so the New Elite do have a talent for consensus politics. They are not, in their own estimation, politicians, an appellation that fills them with disgust. Their opinion of most elected politicians is uncomplimentary in the extreme and they have no time for office politics. This is not to say that they are not masters of office or, at least, boardroom politics themselves. It is just that they will not allow their subordinates to indulge in internecine warfare. It is an attitude that wins the overwhelming approval of people who work for them, who find that the freedom to express their opinions without feeling they may be taken down and used in evidence against them exhilarating and liberating.

Our average chief executive's own office, predictably, is an important work centre. It tends to be a large, well-lit room near the top of the building, rather traditionally furnished in unremarkable colours. There is usually, but not always, a desk, in any case scrupulously clean of papers, while at the other end of the room is a group of sofas and armchairs round a low table, often facing a fireplace above which hangs a portrait of the founder, or a modest land or seascape. The personality of the man himself is singularly lacking. The truth is, of course, that he doesn't care about his working environment, provided it is convenient.

There are no signs of new technology. This is hidden away with his team of secretaries, who are equipped, naturally, with wordprocessors, fax machines, modems and the other paraphernalia of the modern office. Colin Marshall of British Airways has an arrivals and departures screen in his office, so he can see what planes are leaving late, and most have a television and video tucked discreetly away, but the only obvious communications technology is a telephone.

In spite of its anonymity, the office sees quite a lot of its occupant. It abuts those of his close colleagues, with whom he meets as frequently as possible. Most of our chief executives have a tight team of senior directors and executives with whom they relate very closely. The insider team can vary from three or four to upwards of eight or nine, depending in part on the size of the group.

It may come as a surprise to learn that the life of the chief executive of many large companies is a lonely one. In a conventional group it is often the managing directors of the operating divisions who have the power bases. They may report to the chief executive, but it is they who have people and resources under their direct control. They put up their own proposals, which often conflict with counter-arguments from other divisional heads, submit their own budgets and defend their division's performance as though it were their own – which it frequently is. The situation at the top is commonly compared to that between a medieval king and his feudal barons. Like the luckless King John, the chief executive can find himself with only his intellect to pitch against the real power of his nominal subordinates, who can force him into accepting situations he would really like to change.

Some chief executives have tried to counter this situation by bringing in outside consultants or strategic planners of their own, in order to add muscle to their own arguments. But this can compound the problem if the executive directors decide to resent the intruders instead of accepting them as reinforcements.

None of the New Elite has fallen into this trap. One of the fundamental secrets of Peter Walters's success, for example, is the way in which he has transformed the executive directors of BP from independent barons defending their separate fiefdoms into a kind of examining body setting joint standards for the divisions. None of the chief executives we talked to has formally created what in America would be called the 'office of the chief executive'. However, they have all formed some kind of top strategic management group, sometimes only two or three strong and none more than nine.

The role of this group is to debate the future of the company. It is usually very flexible, drawing in executive directors and managers as well as calling on expert advisers, and cutting across formal management structures. It could be described as a think-tank, if this term had not been discredited by governments to suggest ineffectual cerebrations which are either misused as propaganda or disregarded. Nothing could be further from the truth in the case of the New Elite. What the strategy group decides is invariably put into action.

The success of these groups depends on the extent to which they create a genuine forum for debate and the quality of the conclusions they produce. This in turn tends to reflect the intellects and independence of the people whom the chief executive recruits. It is a facet of the New Elite that they are never afraid of subjecting their management ideas to critical appraisal by the brightest brains they can find. The benefits of this tend to be twofold. One is that it helps stop their companies doing silly things. The other is that their proposals are, due to all this high-powered strategic thinking, rather good, which makes everyone else in the company keener to put them into action.

The key, however, is that the executive directors are themselves part of the overall strategy group, so that they share its conclusions. This integration between strategy and operation also protects the New Elite from isolation. This doesn't mean that they are all relentless extroverts. But even the least gregarious never lets himself get out of touch with any of his businesses.

There is a great deal of informal interchange between the members of the top team. Whether they all like having their boss breathing down their necks in the way that the New Elite do is questionable, but if they don't, they have to lump it. One attribute shared by all our chief executives is their persistent curiosity. It's all done in the best possible taste, of course, but they have learned the hard way that knowledge is power.

The end of the working day is all too frequently devoted to 'eating hot dinners', as Sir John Egan of Jaguar resignedly describes the process of dining with important customers or taking part in public events. The New Elite are becoming superstars, always in demand to speak on industrial relations, the state of the nation or the future of the world. They refuse many invitations but are still left with a large number that they accept. Some chief executives are more reluctant than others, as you can tell by looking at the lists of their extra-curricular commitments. People like Sir Trevor Holdsworth of GKN or Sir David Plastow of Vickers obviously can't resist joining anything with Industry in its name. All of them, however, spend a great deal of their out-of-office hours acting as propagandists for their companies and for industry at large.

They don't find it quite the hardship they pretend. After all, even the most introverted people like praise and these men are not introverts. Being fêted is not that unpleasant. And they also enjoy speaking in public; all of them are good communicators and they also have strong opinions – on industrial relations, the state of the nation and the future of the world, as it so happens.

At the end of a long day, however, they like to go home to their families. Judging by the high proportion of their marriages which have survived, being a workaholic high-achiever is not as destructive of personal relationships as might be expected. Perhaps absence makes the heart grow fonder or perhaps it is because, unlike most of us, they love every minute of their working lives.

The Formula for Recovery

It is probably true to say that every chief executive in the industrialized world worth his salt has read *In Search of Excellence: Lessons from America's Best-Run Companies* by Thomas J. Peters and Robert H. Waterman Jnr. No one who has read it can deny that it gives an inspired perspective on modern management methods in the US. There can be no doubt that every top British businessman, including the New Elite, has been impressed, entertained and influenced by it. But it was not published until 1982, by which time all the chief executives we are writing about were already in action. The crunch date for British industry was, we remind you, 1978, when oil prices leapt for the second time in a decade and it became unavoidably apparent to the most inward-looking boards of directors that things were not going to get better by themselves.

The type of industry did not seem to matter. British business was in a bind. Pay, price and exchange controls abounded. Inflation was rampant. Labour was often out of control. The pound was fluctuating in value like a yo-yo. Foreign imports were flooding in and exports were languishing. Profits were vanishing like snow in summer.

British companies were in trouble in almost every area, but particularly in manufacturing industry. It wasn't a surprise to senior management. Everyone knew the reasons. Companies had been struggling to cope with many of the pressures for the last five years, if not longer. It was just that, suddenly, it was obvious that the eleventh hour was long gone and in many cases it was five minutes past midnight.

It was in these circumstances that the New Elite found themselves placed in command. Sometimes they were recruited from outside, like John Egan and Colin Marshall, while David Plastow emerged in the top executive slot as a result of a takeover. In most instances, however, they were promoted internally. They were selected because they had raised their voices in protest against current policies, or lack of them. John Harvey-Jones, for example, had delivered a swingeing attack on ICI's failure to implement a policy of diversification which it had approved at the beginning of the 1970s. Richard Giordano had attacked BOC bitterly in 1977, when he tried to stop the British group taking total control of Airco, its US subsidiary of which he was president. Others were less provocative, but none were less than positive in their views. What they said was not necessarily rejected by their fellow directors. It was Sir Leslie Smith, the previous chairman, who selected Giordano to lead BOC and gave him the exceptional powers to effect change. Peter Walters and John Harvey-Jones were both chosen by their peers, in preference to rivals, because they had the most clearly defined course of action. Some, like Trevor Holdsworth and Sir Stanley Grinstead, succeeded quite conventionally, with few shock waves. Even they, however, had made it crystal clear to their colleagues that things were not going to stay the same.

Not all were formally styled 'chief executive', but a significant proportion were given this American title, instead of the traditional British label of 'managing director'. In every case, however, they were given an unequivocal mandate for change. And in every case they promptly applied the same formula to achieve their ends. As business theories go, it is simple in the extreme. It boils down to concentrating on what the company does best and doing it better.

The actions that the New Elite have taken have not been in themselves revolutionary. In many ways, in fact, they could be said to be simplistic. If you imagine there is some magic involved in their success, you are going to be disappointed. Commonsense might be the noun to use to summarize their approach.

What is striking is that the same formula was applied by every one of the people we investigated. The same principles were used in each case, regardless of the business involved. Managing companies in crisis, it appears, is not a subtle activity.

If you would like a very brief action list, it might be reduced to the following:

Sort out the cash
Sort out the management
Sort out the men
Sort out the product
Sort out the marketing

And, if anybody drags his feet, get rid of him.

That is, of course, a gross over-simplification. The operative word is 'sort'. One of the outstanding characteristics of the New Elite is their ability to win the hearts and minds of the people who work for them. They believe in sweet reason rather than bullying. They pride themselves on listening first and acting afterwards. But it has to be admitted that the steel is never far from the surface. The New Elite may take advice, they may even enter into debates, but they brook no argument. They would not be leaders if they became involved in arguments. And it is leadership which is their outstanding characteristic.

The most immediate step the New Elite took was to bring their companies' finances under control. To a man they say that a company that is not making money is a company that ought to be closed down. Michael Edwardes was perhaps the first exponent of this tenet at BL. You may think it ridiculous that such an obvious fact needed facing, but when Edwardes closed down BL's Speke factory in Liverpool, it was the first shutdown in the British motor car industry for ten years. One of the fundamental weaknesses of British management had been its reluctance to take action to close down inefficient or unprofitable operations, largely through fear of the unions.

It is a moot point whether the New Elite needed the Tory Government's support to outface the unions. It is true that Tory legislation has helped break trades union power. The failure of the mineworkers' strike and the weakness of the print unions in their struggles against new technology and militant newspaper proprietors has shown that. But again, the New Elite managed to effect dramatic reductions in employee numbers before either of these confrontations. The number of jobs that the New Elite have had to eliminate is huge. The average cut was around 30% and several came close to halving their workforces. Some of the jobs went through the sale of unwanted subsidiaries, but most were due to straightforward redundancies and factory closures.

The New Elite are unabashed. The truth is they had long realized the need to cut back on employee numbers. Harvey-Jones recalls an old joke which asked: What is the difference between ICI and British Rail? Answer: ICI has more passengers. BP's bureaucracy was notorious. Jaguar Cars' productivity was down to less than one and a half cars per employee a year.

15

Surprisingly, the employees went remarkably peacefully on the whole. This was largely due to one of the New Elite's fundamental beliefs – the importance of communications. If there is a single aspect in which successful managers differ from the rest, it is in their commitment to telling the workers what is happening.

While the cull was taking place, the new bosses were already putting the rest of their battle plan into action. Most of them started, in fact, by asking what business their companies should be in at all. Again, it sounds ridiculous, pure management school theory. What is the point of BP asking itself what business it should be in? It's got to be oil, hasn't it? Except that with the passage of time almost all big companies manage to acquire the strangest collection of subsidiaries. BOC, for example, had invested in over sixty different businesses, from metal trading to pizzas.

Getting rid of everything except the core businesses was another of the fundamental actions that the New Elite took. The companies they kept were ones that they believed were capable of securing or keeping a major market share. Peter Walters and John Harvey-Jones actually swapped BP's PVC company for ICI's polythene division as a shortcut to beefing up both businesses. They called it a variety of names. Market re-orientation is one. What it boiled down to in most cases was drastically reducing the group's total size and turnover. Sales sometimes fell as sharply as employee numbers.

The surgery was so extensive that for a short time people wondered whether the patients would survive. The New Elite, however, never doubted the need to cut deeply into the fatty tissues. That they were right was proved gratifyingly fast. Profits recovered and the immediate financial problems rolled back. But this was, to our heroes, just the starting point.

Their third objective has been to revitalize the management structures in their companies. It wasn't just the numbers that they objected to; it was also their belief that far too many people were doing superfluous jobs, particularly in head office. If you are looking for a seminal influence on this line of thinking, it could be Robert Townsend's *Up the Organization*. Colin Marshall is a particular admirer of Townsend because they both used to work for Avis, but the American's message – get rid of unnecessary staff functions and cut out hierarchical systems – is profoundly believed by all the New Elite.

Once again, what they have done sounds deceptively simple. It is to push responsibility firmly on to the shoulders of the people in charge of the group's operating companies and then to make them as directly answerable to the chief executive as possible. It has resulted, in some cases, in an extraordinary number of layers of intermediate management disappearing. At ICI, it was calculated that as many as sixteen people could stand between the man on the shop floor and the chairman. Harvey-Jones, as an ex-sailor with a profound belief in close relationships with the men under his command, has pruned ICI's bureaucracy with the zest of a commercial Robespierre.

Like their other actions, putting responsibility where it should be, with the man in charge of the job, is easier to describe than to do. For a start it involved sorting the sheep from the goats. Chief executives divide their management into two categories: staff men and line management. Both have their functions, but line managers are the leaders, the doers, the makers. Making sure that the line jobs are not filled by staff men is a fetish of all our chief executives, all of whom bemoan the shortage of leadership talent available.

They are all line managers themselves, of course, by nature and by training. In fact they are the best, which may be one reason why they find so few others who match up to their standards. It is not for want of trying. Michael Edwardes, for example, puts his managers through psychological tests to see how many are round pegs in square holes. But even he does not rely on these tests to decide who is right for what job. In the end it comes down to personal selection. One of the secrets of the New Elite's successes is the care they devote to picking good line managers.

Intriguingly, there are probably fewer casualties at senior levels in the good companies than there are in the bad – at least, once the initial bloodletting is over. The people left have been sorted into the right pigeonholes and are therefore happier and more effective. It must also be true that successful teams tend to trust and support each other. Success breeds success. It also engenders the confidence to try new ideas, to branch out and take risks, especially when the man at the top is consciously encouraging opportunism and new ideas. The ability to pick the right men to run the operating companies perhaps comes down to the old adage: it takes one to know one. That is certainly one of the essential secrets of the New Elite.

They have also gone to considerable lengths to encourage everyone to work harder. One of the ways they have done this was mentioned in passing earlier on: better communications. The New Elite take communications ever more seriously. Internally, they encourage team briefings, regular reports to employees, company newspapers, in-company videos, open days for families, information programmes, any means of letting the workers know what is happening and making them feel it is worth their while helping the company to do better. Other companies set out to do the same thing. The difference here is that the chief executive insists that it really happens, that information does percolate down – and up!

The other incentive in which the New Elite believe as much if not more is reward! Money! They are almost without exception high payers. They are dedicated to raising the salaries of their colleagues, both at basic levels and through incentives for achievement. The view that if you want to attract the best people, you have to pay the best rates, is one in which they can find no flaw. Naturally it applies to them, too. Richard Giordano is no whit abashed because he is paid something like £17,000 a week. John Egan says categorically that he thinks the highest paid people in the country should be the leaders of successful companies; how else can Britain convince its brightest brains to go into industry and help create the wealth on which we all ultimately depend?

The management sorted out, the New Elite turned their attentions to the products. Here the watchwords have been quality, cost effect-iveness and making what the customers want. What John Egan has achieved at Jaguar is a classic example of how to restore consumer trust in a basically good product, which had been allowed to fall into disrepute because of sloppy workmanship and general carelessness about quality and service.

Concentration on quality is a hallmark of the New Elite at work. It can be seen at any level – in the technological excellence of GKN's ubiquitous front wheel drive units to the transformation in British Airways' attitude to passengers. There is no secret here; just an unre-mitting demand for good workmanship, attention to detail, prompt delivery and unstinting after-sales service. It is all part of the New Elite's recognition that, in the final analysis, it is the customer who calls the tune.

The final strand in the formula that has so transformed Britain's better companies is the only one that can really be dignified with the word strategy. It can be summed up in one word: international. Each and every one of the chief executives we talked to stressed the same point. If a company is not competing in world markets, it is doomed. The British market is not large enough. And it is worth noting that they all spoke from experience gained overseas.

The good news is that they have all succeeded. Vickers, for example, is manufacturing in Japan. Courtaulds has a paint factory in China. Grand Metropolitan is almost as big in the US as it is in the UK. GKN supplies parts to most of the car manufacturers in the world. They have achieved their new success by ruthlessly concentrating on products and markets where they have a special edge, either because they are big or because they are selling something that no one else can beat. And they have backed up these products with better marketing, increased research and development, and competitive prices.

It has worked wonderfully. Well, perhaps not wonderfully. The last seven years have seen a frighteningly large percentage of British industry vanish. But some has survived, thanks to new management realism and drive. No one pretends the medicine has been pleasant, but it has worked.

The View from the Top

The New Elite would not be able to operate as efficiently as they do if they did not have a crystal clear mental image of the world in which their companies trade. You could call it an economic model, but it is doubtful that they would. There is nothing abstract about the view they have of society today. Few chief executives, we would guess, have any time for existentialism. Nor do they waste any time in wishful thinking about how to change society.

Perhaps one of the most important points to appreciate about the men who are our heroes is that they are not radicals, let alone revolutionaries. It is notable how little they have to say about politics, about religion, about social change in its widest sense. They are not interested in changing the world; on the contrary, their whole endeavour and their great talent is making the best of things as they are. The outstanding characteristic of the good chief executive, in a word, is pragmatism.

This is rather bad news for anyone who hopes that the problems of Britain's economy can be solved by some magic formula. The only formulae that our chief executives believe in come out of their own research and development and even these, they know from experience, only have limited lives before the competition comes up with an equally good alternative. It is significant that most businessmen are much keener on applied than pure research. They prefer to use the word 'innovation' to 'invention'. Anything totally new is useless until someone has worked out how to make it into a marketable commodity, which could take forever.

If you look at what the New Elite have achieved, it has to be admitted that a great part of it is due more to pruning than planting. They have sold more companies than they have bought, they have cut more products than they have introduced, and they have fired far more people than they have hired. Desperate times require desperate remedies, of course, and no one can deny that half a loaf is better than none. If the New Elite have at best been restorers rather than builders, it is no more than a reflection of what their companies needed. What is remarkable about them is the way in which they take their policies to their logical conclusions. This is, perhaps, what makes the difference between success and failure.

We have found little evidence that the chief executives in our sample are more optimistic than those of most British companies. If anything, it could be said that they are less encouraging about the future for the UK than most. This is not because they are pessimists themselves. Far from it. The New Elite are assiduous at unpicking the linings of worn-out industry in the search for loose silver and always make the best of things.

But they have clearly decided that the future lies outside the UK. It could be said that the best of British industry is busy going off-shore, leaving the rest of us behind. Although all the businessmen we talked to are patriotic, it is difficult to deny that they put their companies first and their country second. One of the fundamental business precepts of the New Elite is the vital importance of being competitive in international markets. They believe that the alternative to being a multinational business is eventual failure. There is a great deal of evidence to support this argument.

All our chief executives like to think of themselves as strategists, as we mentioned earlier. They look at least five years ahead and, if pressed, would admit to thinking as much as ten or fifteen years into the future. However, it might be more accurate to describe their vision as keen rather than wide. The scenarios they paint are all based on the premise that industrialized society will remain basically the same in the foreseeable future.

They are right. Things do tend to go on much as they did before for longer than anyone would believe possible. Everything anticipated in the UK, as in most countries in the world, is based on the assumption that we will need more, rather than less, of the same. No one is planning for radical change and indeed the investments that our society is making now, in the production of new but still the same kind of roads, houses, cars, aeroplanes, food and fashions, is committing industry to making the same kind of products, more or less, at least up to the end of this century.

Revolutionary change is, of course, possible, but it is irrelevant to running a business. Let's face it, the most likely post-industrial society is post the Bomb. And anyway, if you are a businessman, there is absolutely no point in planning for a future in which capitalism is non-existent. From a chief executive's point of view, this may not be the best of all possible worlds, but it is the only world worth thinking about.

It is a world which they deem capable of looking after itself. The New Elite are not overly concerned with the environment. Pollution is a relative matter. Peter Walters, for example, says that the standards of purity and cleanliness demanded by West Germany for any industrial discharges into the Rhine are far greater than the UK needs to impose for effluent going into the North Sea, because the ocean is so much more capable of absorbing undesirable waste.

He is perfectly right, of course, but you see what we mean about limited perspectives. It is probable that most industrialists feel that far too much is asked of them in terms of maintaining, and paying for, unrealistically high standards of cleanliness and safety. They don't like being cast as the bad guys. If Britain wants its industry to produce less pollution than other European countries, for example, the attitude of most industrialists is that the government or society at large must be prepared to pay the cost. The burden should not be lumped on to companies, unless they can be protected against the loss of competitiveness that is involved.

Global arguments about the cumulative effect of acid rain or carbon monoxide build-up in the atmosphere cut little ice. They might be prepared to debate them in the abstract, but don't be surprised if their underlying indifference shows through. What is important is the reality of doing business in a competitive world where the only values are relative.

This underlying belief that the world is a materialist battleground has the virtue of being remarkably free of cant. The New Elite are not bigots, either religious or racial. They are not snobs. They respect talent, hard work and ingenuity, and genuinely think of themselves as egalitarian. However, they do not show much sympathy for the underprivileged. Not in practical terms, anyway. They all profess unhappiness at the numbers whom they have been forced to put out of work, but it hasn't stopped them for a moment.

There is a streak of selfishness running through their personal philosophies that enables them to take hard decisions whatever the cost in human terms. But to suggest that they have any alternative would cause them much indignation. They are only doing their jobs.

Most of the New Elite, to be fair, do speak out on the need for change in British society. They are very critical of the failings of our educational system, but the changes they want tend towards better training for future jobs rather than any radical shift towards equipping the young to live in a jobless society. Bring back the grammar school ethos might summarize their basic opinion. It is a view shared by a large number of people, but it is essentially reactionary. It could almost be described as neo-Victorian. The work ethic ranks high in the morality of the New Elite, but only as the best method of succeeding, either individually or collectively. Their very pragmatism makes them aware of the human race in Darwinist terms, locked in an evolutionary struggle in which only the fittest will survive. Seen through the eyes of the New Elite, it is a hard world in which only the successful can afford to be charitable.

They are a charitable bunch of people themselves. They give generously of their spare energies and money to a wide variety of deserving causes. In particular they try to inspire positive developments in British industry, so that others can benefit from their own experience. They work for the Confederation of British Industry and the British Institute of Management and speak at the annual conference of the Institute of Directors, dispensing words of wisdom, warning and comfort to all those with ears to hear.

This willingness to preach industrial salvation would appear to conflict with our rather cruel definition of the New Elite as detached exploiters of capitalist reality. But then we never said they were simple people. On the contrary.

Ten of the Best

When it came to selecting a representative sample of chief executives, our criteria were, to be honest, less than scientific. By and large we confined ourselves to manufacturing industry, because this is the front line, where the real struggle for survival has been taking place. This is not to dismiss retailing or service industries as less important, but they deserve books of their own.

All our chief executives are managers. That is to say they are employees, like most of us. We have consciously excluded anyone who might be better described as an entrepreneur. It is, we admit, a fine distinction, but we think a relevant one. Each of the people we profile in the succeeding chapters has worked his way up the management ladder. As such, we think they are examples that other aspiring managers can hope to emulate as well as admire.

All their companies are large. Their size varies considerably from the Chloride Group with a turnover of a mere £400m to BP with £40 billion, but collectively they represent a significant slice of the UK's entire industrial output. Most importantly, all of them have triumphed in bitter battles for the survival of their companies. Let's face it, they are all winners and that is our real reason for choosing them. They are the best.

When it came to deciding in what order to place our profiles, we found ourselves at a loss. We hope you will find that each chapter illustrates different aspects of company leadership, but deciding any order of merit proved impossible. We did, in fact, ask our sample who they would choose as the best chief executive in the UK. We were told in no uncertain terms that it was a silly question. Each of the people we portray has responded to the individual circumstances that his company faced. These have varied so greatly that comparison is clearly invidious. So in the end we have taken the only option left to us and put the New Elite in alphabetical order.

The Missionary

MICHAEL OWEN EDWARDES
Chairman: The Chloride Group plc

Born 11 October 1930
Marriage dissolved – three daughters

Education:
St Andrew's College, Grahamstown, South Africa
BA, Rhodes University, Grahamstown

Business career:
Chloride Group 1951 (ongoing involvement)
BL 1977–82
Mercury Communications 1982–3
ICL 1984
Dunlop Holdings 1984–5
Non-executive director: Hill Samuel Group; Gooding
Group; Minerals and Resources Corp.; Stabilization
Ltd; International Management Development Institute
(USA)

Sir Michael Edwardes is the natural starting point for any study of chief executives in the United Kingdom. He stands unchallenged as the best-known industrial leader in the UK, the man who tackled the job that couldn't be done at BL, the man who broke the power of the unions, the man whom other managers either love or hate.

It is surprising what strong emotions Michael Edwardes arouses in his peers. His admirers are only rivalled in numbers by his detractors. For every chief executive who considers Edwardes as the man who above all others restored the right of British managers to manage, there is another who damns his achievements with faint praise. The most common criticism is that he is only good at confrontation and that he is not a wealth creator.

Michael Edwardes's five years at BL were a mission impossible; the mere fact that the British car manufacturer emerged alive is next to miraculous. Edwardes has chronicled those years in his own book *Back from the Brink*. In this book he also details something of his early years in South Africa as the son of a Welsh emigrant motor dealer with a belief in self-improvement. Michael Edwardes's obsessive pursuit of excellence owes much to his father's uncompromising attitudes towards achievement. Edwardes's account of spending a week recovering a lost outboard motor before he dared return home, is the stuff of which heroes are tempered in childhood.

Whether any child can be envied for having such a demanding parent is another question. There is a brittle quality about Edwardes even now that suggests an instinctive defensiveness. His reaction to people he does not know can appear almost paranoid. He has a trick of fixing strangers with an unblinking stare until they are introduced and explained, like a mongoose eyeing a snake. And he is equally cautious in conversation, always careful to define his own level of commitment before volunteering any contribution.

He is almost painfully intense. He rarely smiles; not because he is without humour, but because jokes equate with flippancy and Edwardes is hardly ever flippant. He is too busy. Rudyard Kipling's verse:

If you can fill the unforgiving minute
With sixty seconds' worth of distance run,
Yours is the Earth and everything that's in it,
And – which is more – you'll be a Man, my son!

could have been written with Edwardes in mind.

But this is just the outside casing. To those who work with him, Michael Edwardes can be a revelation. Take, for example, his recent sojourn as chief executive of Dunlop. To the public at large, Edwardes's involvement was most notable for the publicity surrounding the huge share options which were granted to him in the rescue package he masterminded. This concession proved to be a public relations disaster, although it is doubtful whether it had real bearing on the subsequent takeover of Dunlop by BTR. It certainly reflected Michael Edwardes's desire to become rich, but it was not really unusual. Other executives have become multi-millionaires as a reward for rescuing ailing groups. John Beckett, who made at least £3m out of the resurgence of Woolworth's is just one example.

What was less widely appreciated outside was the incredible impact Edwardes had on Dunlop's morale in the weeks he was in charge in late 1984 and early 1985. The Edwardes magic was at its most apparent in his visits to Dunlop plants. On his first trip outside the London head office of the beleaguered rubber group, he chose a Coventry factory, where admittedly his name was very well known due to his long struggle with BL. Even so, his reception was extraordinary. In his progress round the plant he was greeted like a cross between Royalty and a filmstar. The workers' belief in his ability to save the company and their jobs was almost tangible.

Edwardes played up to this hero image. He has very clearly developed ideas about the role of the chief executive as leader, ideas which he has tested to the limit at BL. There is no other industrialist in the UK who has so dauntlessly put himself in the front line.

The visit to Coventry was mostly for show. Significant changes had already taken place in the group. Edwardes's first action as chief executive of Dunlop had been to subject its top 200 executives to a shock reassessment of their suitability for their jobs by submitting them to a series of psychological tests.

'We all went off to the Charing Cross Road for a whole day of IQ tests,' one of the managers involved recalls. 'It was quite fun really, although a lot of people found it rather frightening as well. In fact Sir Michael responded to the results mostly by moving people. Mostly they were men who had been promoted beyond their capabilities. He always maintained that the tests were only part of his assessment. He was really trying to find out how self-motivated people were.'

It was not the first time that Edwardes had tested his new management in this way. He had done the same at ICL, where he became chairman directly after leaving BL. There, he says, they were taken for granted. 'American companies use them all the time,' he adds, as though that is total justification.

Edwardes believes deeply that one of the overriding problems of British industry is having too many people in the wrong jobs. Managers, he has said, are more concerned with saving face than with doing what has to be done. They wallow in consensus and accept compromise as a matter of course.

His own achievement as a leader is his ability to draw startlingly good performances out of people who previously have been doing most things wrong. It is what he began doing in his brief period at Dunlop and it is the hallmark of his efforts at BL. But it is a talent which dates back to his previous career at the Chloride Group.

Edwardes's years at Chloride have been overshadowed by his more recent exploits, but they were the foundation on which all his subsequent actions have been based. It is almost a shock to discover that he has worked for Chloride for most of his adult life. He was recruited by the British battery manufacturer for a two-year training programme in the UK in 1951, when he was twenty, a budding entrepreneur fresh out of university in South Africa. He spent the time working for one of Chloride's most dynamic figures, Charles Cook, whose approach to getting on with the job was exactly in line with his own.

For most of his first fifteen years at Chloride, Edwardes worked in Africa, first building up its small Rhodesian operation and then gradually expanding sales across the continent. Africa was a very different place in those days, with the drive towards independence and the rejection of British influence only gathering pace, and the scope for individual initiative was still considerable.

When Edwardes arrived in the UK to stay in 1966, it was as commercial director of Chloride's smallest subsidiary, Alkaline Batteries. He was thirty-five, which was in no way exceptionally young for a senior job in a company only just making money. But within a year he was general manager, from which point the change in the fortunes of Alkaline was extraordinary. It was there Edwardes demonstrated for the first time his gift for winning the loyalty of competent executives through whom he is able to achieve so much so quickly. The apparently superhuman capacity of all successful chief executives is, in the end, due to this talent to delegate, which, in turn, is copied by their subordinates. The ripple effect on productivity can be extraordinary.

At Alkaline, Edwardes recruited several young executives from outside the group and formed a dedicated, close-knit, youthful team, which began running the company with business school intensity, 'as if engaged in some protracted management game', as *Management Today* described it in 1975. Edwardes cut the workforce by 260, redesigned and repackaged the products, and began a sales drive for new business around the world. Within two years Alkaline Batteries was humming and Edwardes, then thirty-nine, was invited to join Chloride's main board.

Eighteen months later he was put in charge of Chloride's biggest headache, Electric Power Storage, which made the group's lead-acid batteries, selling most of its output to the car industry and employing a quarter of Chloride's total workforce. In deep financial trouble, EPS had failed to capitalize on the closure of one of its major factories and was losing money heavily.

Edwardes chopped through EPS's problems by dividing it into two companies: one supplying the motor industry and the other concentrating on other markets. He also gave Chloride a new European direction, buying distributors in France and Belgium and starting up a grass-roots operation in Germany in direct competition with the powerful Varta battery company.

By then he was chief executive of the whole group, only a year and a half after being given control of EPS. The appointment was a direct reflection of his outstanding performance. He was promoted from among forty theoretically equally senior executives in Chloride, although in reality he already had charge of a quarter of the group. His success in resolving the problems passed on to him had made his promotion inevitable. What marked out Edwardes from the rest was his ability to make things happen. More than anything else, he had shown that he could define the real target and then hit it.

Helping him drive Chloride ever upwards to new sales and profit records were his hand-picked Alkaline team, whose members had followed their patron into the higher echelons of the group like missionaries to the unconverted tribes. They were also joined by more newcomers from outside.

Edwardes has always been ready to buy in managerial talent when it is needed. Within four years of taking over control at Chloride, one in three of its top one hundred managers had been recruited from outside, an extremely high turnover for a mature group. He is also completely ruthless about sorting the sheep from the goats. 'One of the besetting sins of British industry', he emphasizes, 'is the number of intelligent staff people in line jobs.' It is something that he never allows to last.

Predictably, Edwardes saw the oil crisis in 1973 as a great opportunity for Chloride. By multiplying the cost of diesel and petrol, it transformed the economics of alternative power sources. Suddenly, the prospect of competitive battery-powered vehicles seemed credible. It inspired Chloride into a major expansion into the United States with the takeover of Connrex Corporation of Tampa, Florida, America's seventh largest battery maker.

Edwardes also launched Chloride on an intensive quest for more efficient batteries, which is still testing its patience to the limit today. For the last ten years Chloride has been striving to perfect a sodium sulphur battery with greatly enhanced power capability. Edwardes himself has never lost faith in the product, but he admits that there have been times when Chloride has been close to pulling the plug on the research and development programme.

If it had, he would not have complained. 'Courage', he says, 'is essential to leadership, but there is a difference between bravery and sheer bloody-mindedness. I don't think staying with something regardless of the facts is very clever.' But throughout his commitment to Chloride, which has continued in a non-executive capacity side by side with his other jobs, he has stayed loyal to sodium sulphur battery research. Today it perches tantalizingly on the verge of startling success, promising a battery five times as powerful as conventional lead acid batteries and a revolution in urban transport.

Edwardes is one of those people who, deep down inside, believe that nothing worth doing is easy. There is a streak of romance running through him which is probably shared by almost every chief executive worth his salt and which, in the final analysis, is the conviction that there really is a pot of gold at the end of the industrial rainbow.

When Michael Edwardes agreed to move into the hot seat at BL, Chloride's turnover had multiplied five times to £260m and profits were up seven times to £26m. Ironically, the group's almost perfect industrial relations record was marred by a nine-week strike only months before its chief executive's departure to tackle the worst industrial relations job in the UK. The strike was caused, on the surface, by Edwardes's attempt to formalize a productivity agreement which until then had been largely unwritten. What the workforce feared was the very thing the management believed would guarantee Chloride success, namely its expansion into international operations. British workmen have always suspected overseas investment as the thin end of a wedge that will be used either to reduce their wages or to destroy their jobs entirely. It is a fear not without substance.

Edwardes is not a supporter of legislating industrial relations. 'What about the Industrial Relations Bill?' he was asked before it was enacted. 'So far as we are concerned, it should be locked away in a safe place and forgotten,' he replied trenchantly, although he did add that he would not be willing to be at variance with the law if he found himself in conflict with it. His own solution to employee relations has always been what he calls 'participation'. As soon as information can be divulged, he believes in telling as many people as possible, so that they are involved. Participation is, he says, not a style of management, it is a way of life.

This belief is one of the reasons why he found himself totally opposed to BL's shop stewards. He became convinced that they were acting with malice aforethought to deny BL's workers the facts and were intentionally subverting communication channels to intensify confrontation with management. As proof, he cites the ultimate confrontation between the BL board and the unions over his dismissal of Derek 'Red Robbo' Robinson, the Austin Rover shop steward.

It was only because some of us went over the heads of these militants to the employees that we started to learn that they were as browned off with the environment as the managers. That was the truth that emerged which no one in 1977 would have believed. If I had said then, when the massive strikes were taking place in the UK car industry, that all these people really wanted to be at work, I would have been thought crazy. In fact, it was true. The minute firm management came in there was a great response. This was finally demonstrated in the Derek Robinson case. One must never forget that out of 14,000 people that day at that great open-air meeting at Austin Rover, only 400 voted for him.

But Michael Edwardes is the first to admit that firm management is not in itself enough. There also has to be a leader:

There does seem to be a particular sort of chemistry which can't easily be defined, which can't easily be emulated or copied, but which enables certain people to lead companies. What is it that enables John Harvey-Jones to make a fairly sleepy ICI take off? What enables John Egan to take a company that was in a fair mess when I invited him to come in and grab it by the scruff of the neck, shake it and sort it out in short order?

I can tell you very clearly what the answer to that is. It is nothing to do with administrative ability. It isn't to do with theoretical competence. It's to do with straight leadership.

The leader sees what is wrong and he does that by hearing what is wrong, by talking to people, by listening. A good leader actually listens an awful lot. Politicians should take note of this.

What have they got in common? They are not petty. Very important. All of them are shrewd enough to see that other people can be of help to them. In other words, they are team players. Some are extrovert, some are not, but nevertheless, they all have a magic in terms of their perception of problems. They know how to inspire people to sort out those problems. All this is to do with an inner intuitiveness. And they have a particular drive, a desire to bring order out of chaos, or if something is too cosy, to create chaos in order to bring about change.

They have this driving force inside them and people follow them because they inspire trust. They create confidence that they know what they are doing. And once people begin to follow, the horse-power is enormous. The good leader is someone who is followed, rather than someone who obtrusively leads. People make the leader;

he doesn't make himself. They recognize that he has a mission and they trust him to achieve it.

Nothing in the world will persuade me that this talent can be inculcated into a man in a business school or by some other external means. It is absolutely inherent in the man. And then, of course, the experience the man acquires, the nature and complexity of the problems he faces, make him a more and more powerful leader or otherwise, as the case may be.

In some ways Edwardes says it is more difficult if the new leader is already part of the company when he takes over. 'Bringing about change can then be quite difficult because people take you for granted. When you come in from outside, you have far more leverage to create change, because you are an unknown factor and people are going to take you more seriously than if they have grown up with you. On the other hand, you do not have the deep knowledge of the business.'

The first thing a leader does, Edwardes says, is set standards for his executives considerably higher than existed previously. 'That is one sign of a leader: that he sets fences for colleagues to jump that they did not know they could clear. In a very big company there is enough competence floating around, enough administrative ability, enough people who understand the legal or financial aspects. The top chap has to be a generalist and he has to lead.'

Edwardes feels that British managers perform very well outside Britain, whereas all managers in Britain find it difficult. 'Quite a lot of top-flight Germans and Americans and others – I can think of people in the motor industry who have come and gone – have no more than dented some of the problems. Whenever you hear me decrying British management, I don't actually mean that managers who are British are not any good. It is just that in this country they prove to be inadequate to the task. All of us come across problems that we can't resolve in the British scene.'

His views on strategy are simple:

Leaders operate like a double-barrelled shotgun, with a choke barrel and a non-choke barrel. One barrel is what they use to deal with immediate and urgent problems, like I did at BL. In those situations you put strategy a little bit on a back burner while you deal with crucial and immediate problems. Your second barrel is the strategic one.

35

The barrels, of course, using the same analogy, have to be pointing in the same direction. If your strategic barrel points off at an angle, you can shoot someone you regret.

I believe that supreme commonsense is worth a great deal more than intellect. I can think of people in other countries, particularly in the United States, who may not have been particularly clever, but who have proved extremely effective as managers because they have a great deal of commonsense allied with a lot of drive. And, very importantly, they have surrounded themselves with some key staff with high intellectual abilities who have cracked problems for them.

These are not yes-men. There has to be grit in the oyster to make a pearl. These chaps reporting to the chief executive have to be their own men and have credibility and authority. Otherwise again a big company won't operate effectively.

At BL, Edwardes adopted a very high profile, but he does not believe the public image of the leader is as critical as many might imagine. In a well-managed, orderly company, he says, visibility is not always necessary and he prefers the man who chairs the board in a calm, quiet way, persuading his colleagues without getting in the newspapers every day. A public leader is not a *sine qua non* for a successful company, but in the situation he found at BL, high visibility was necessary:

In order to deal with the very public problems that were coming up, unless I had high visibility, we wouldn't have had politicians taking the board seriously. There is no question but that keeping politicians off the back of the BL board was a very big part of my five years there. There was no way we could have taken on the militants on the shopfloor without matching them on the *Today* programme. Our case was often going by default at seven o'clock in the morning. The media grab these people. The BL situation of 1978–9 was not, however, hopefully the way normal business operates. We had an incredible environment when you think back on it.

He found it virtually impossible to move out of the role when it was no longer necessary: 'Indeed, I came to the conclusion after five years that the only way to change the style at BL was for me to go, because the media had run with me to such an extent there was no way I could reverse it. I felt I would be an Aunt Sally to be shot at for as long as I was there.'

He had also begun to run out of steam himself. Edwardes is, like most men of his type, almost inexhaustible. He is extremely fit – he is still an avid squash player with a speed around the court disconcerting for a man in his mid-fifties – and he has never stinted the time he has given to any of the businesses for which he has worked. Perhaps, however, BL revenged itself on its saviour in the end. He is the only one of our sample of business leaders whose marriage has ended in divorce. This was not entirely due to his overwhelming involvement in the rescue of the car group, but undoubtedly a contributing factor. His private life has also been indelibly marked by public exposure.

It is probable that he has always striven to impose his physical presence, partly because he is shorter than average and partly because of a strong need to command total attention at all times. At BL, however, he became an actor in the grand manner, a master of the effective entrance and a conscious manipulator of the corporate stage. At press conferences, he learned always to enter last, so that every eye centred on him and, as the moment to take the stage approached, he closed in on himself as he took on his role as the leading man.

It may be, too, that he has felt a certain sense of anticlimax since BL, although he can hardly be said to have lacked subsequent parts. He had hardly left the car company before he was in the hot seat at ICL, followed only too quickly by another fire-fighting job at Dunlop. Both were rescue operations, the latter more extreme than the former. Edwardes did not have time in either job to prove himself or his formula for recovery before someone else took over. Especially at Dunlop, however, his survival plan drew admiration from everyone involved, and it has been openly plagiarized by the man who snatched the group away from him, Sir Owen Green of BTR.

Today the wheel has turned full circle and Michael Edwardes is once again in effective charge of the Chloride Group. He had retained his links with the group throughout his BL adventure and returned to the board as non-executive chairman in 1983. In his absence, Chloride's fortunes had fallen into a sad decline. In 1978, the year after Edwardes left, profits rose to £36m, but then collapsed and have languished ever since. Better proof that Edwardes was responsible for Chloride's previous achievements would be hard to find, although his critics say that the company was reaping what he had sown.

It is true that Edwardes would have found it difficult to maintain his company's dramatic growth pattern. The second oil price crisis, the high value of sterling, runaway inflation and high interest rates affected every British company. On the other hand, there can be no doubt that he would have run Chloride differently. Early in December 1985, in his capacity as non-executive chairman, he announced that his current successor as chief executive was relinquishing the job in the light of Chloride's continuing problems, particularly in the USA, where almost all Edwardes's own expansionist acquisitions have had to be sold off, ironically to Dunlop. A search for a new chief executive was begun, but in the meantime Edwardes took the chair of the Group Management Board. In other words, he was taking over executive power again.

It was, perhaps, inevitable. Sir Michael is not cut out to sit idly by at the head of a table. It could be some time before someone capable of filling the Mighty Atom's shoes at Chloride is discovered and, in the meantime, there will be another chance to see one of British industry's all-time stars leading a company back from the wilderness.

The Capitalist Hero

JOHN LEOPOLD EGAN
Chairman and Chief Executive: Jaguar Cars plc

Born 7 November 1939
Married – two daughters

Education:
Bablake School, Coventry
BSc Petroleum Engineering, Imperial College, London
MSc Business Studies, London Business School

Business career:
Bahrein Petroleum Co. 1961–2
Shell International 1962–6
General Motors 1968–71
British Leyland 1971–6
Massey-Ferguson 1976–80
Jaguar Cars 1980–
Non-executive director: Foreign & Colonial Investment
Trust

Of all chief executives in Britain today, John Egan is the most perfect example of the capitalist hero, *sans peur et sans reproche.* His success at Jaguar Cars is the nearest thing to an Arthurian Knightly quest that modern industrial society is capable of producing.

Egan looks as though he could have coped with the rigours of medieval chivalry. He has the rugged appearance of an intelligent brawler, his nose corrugated by rugby accidents, his crisp greying hair cropped close to his large skull and his solid figure reflecting his daily pre-breakfast run. He would have made a good baron. After all, Arthur's knights were just an earlier example of tough bosses trying to hold together a beleaguered economy in the face of foreign competition.

John Egan's achievement at Jaguar has an importance out of proportion to the firm's financial size. Jaguar Cars is, compared to BP, ICI, Grand Metropolitan and other major groups, a small company. It is a single product business employing only about 11,000 people and its sales of around 40,000 cars a year are worth less than £1 billion. But it is a standard-bearer for British excellence around the world and a shining example of this country's ability to rival the best that the Germans, Japanese and Americans can produce in terms of quality and service. Like all outstanding reputations, Jaguar's is a little oversold, but that, too, is a measure of Egan's success. Recreating the legend of Jaguar has been a conscious part of Egan's strategy. The myth of Jaguar supremacy has been as vigorously propagated as Merlin's magical powers, with equally impressive results.

It only takes a visit to any Jaguar showroom to see how the Jaguar image has been extended to create a total ambience of upmarket style. Jaguar's customers want their cars to make a personal statement about their own wealth, power and style. Egan has carefully and meticulously pandered to this demand. Just sitting in a Jaguar is an ego trip, with its real leather upholstery, its walnut panelling and its handcrafted feel. But added on are all the accessories, the personalized sunglasses, keyrings, driving coats, pullovers, briefcases, picnic rugs, watches, ties, belts, jewellery, wallets ... perhaps the wallets should be given away free with every Jaguar bought.

Egan has also taken Jaguar into racing, hiring the ultra-competitive Tom Walkinshaw to manage its onslaught on the reputations of Mercedes, Porsche and BMW, which are its main rivals. Not, of course, in Formula One, but in the sophisticated road races like the Le Mans Twenty-four Hours.

Jaguar, says Egan, is not yet the best car in the world, but it is very near to being what he wants it to be, the ideal car in which to drive from London to Monaco, speeding effortlessly down the French autoroutes into Provence, finally to toss the keys nonchalantly to the doorman at Monte Carlo's Hôtel de Paris.

The fact that he is so near to his objectives only highlights Egan's achievements at Jaguar since he took over as chief executive in May 1980 at the request of Sir Michael Edwardes. Perhaps 'request' is understating it a little. Edwardes wooed Egan hard. He had in fact asked him to join BL two years before, but Egan thought Edwardes was being unrealistic about how much of BL could be saved. He had had previous experience of the group as the head and virtual creator of Unipart, the spares division, and he had become deeply disillusioned about its prospects.

I was recruited to what was then British Leyland Overseas in 1971. I was actually hired by John Barber, of whom I had heard quite a lot at the London Business School. The general feeling at the time was that he was doing quite a good job at BLMC.

Egan's spell at the London Business School had been between 1966 and 1968. 'It was a marvellous experience, because it was the first Master's course in London. The whole place had not shaken down and it was very exciting. There were some extremely talented people; Jim Ball was in charge of the MSc programme and Terry Burns was doing research, and there were lots of very intelligent people on the first course.'

Egan was twenty-six, but that did not inhibit him from joining in the criticism of the courses, which were in a formative stage. Egan was on the joint council of students and faculty that assessed the

43

effectiveness of the lessons, with the Business School fairly quick to react:

> I learned that none of the disciplines, like accounting or market research, or production engineering or whatever, were holy cows. I've had the awareness ever since, whenever I deal with experts in any discipline, that I don't feel they are superior to me. I found that of tremendous use when Jaguar was privatizing, when we were going into areas we had not experienced before. I used to say to my colleagues that we would find it quite easy when we got used to it. I used to call it poking about with a white stick. I remember people being terrified that our accounting systems would not measure up to the Stock Exchange's Long Form Report, but we sailed through that with no trouble at all.

Egan had quit his job as a petroleum engineer with Shell to go to business school:

> I suppose I was lucky in my first job. At school [Bablake Grammar School, Coventry] I was a prefect and that sort of thing, but I was never captain of school or the cricket team. I was quite individualistic. The same was true at university. I don't think I ever ran a society or anything like that. I became a petroleum engineer because a friend of mine had gone to Imperial College and said the rugby was good. I rather fancied that.

Egan's battered nose is a memento of his sporting days. He picked petroleum engineering because the same friend said the Royal School of Mines was the most enjoyable part of Imperial College. Egan was a member of the Chaps Club, a beer-drinking fraternity which demands that its members wear a particularly unattractive brown and blue tie on Fridays. Any member caught without his tie is liable to buy drinks for all the chaps who catch him out. 'I still get fellows coming up to me all round the world wearing those wretched ties and demanding drinks.'

His first job with Bahrein Petroleum immediately called on untested powers of leadership. Within days of arriving in Bahrein, Egan found himself in charge of three teams of Arabs, about fifty men in all, under three gangpushers, only two of whom spoke any English. Without his direct presence nobody did any work. 'I remember one occasion when I overslept. We started at 5.30 in the morning and I'd been up late the night before. When I arrived at the headquarters, everyone else had gone but my three gangs were camped out in front of the manager's window, brewing up. The manager was furious. "Making tea in front of my office!" he shouted at me.'

Egan worked for Shell for nearly five years, on a variety of jobs in the field from the desert to offshore oil rigs. As he grew more experienced, he became increasingly involved in forward exploration planning and became aware that he was going to need different skills if he was to become, as he was clearly destined to be, a manager as well as an engineer:

> I remember having to do calculations on what the net return would be on a small exploration venture almost as though it were from a cookery book. I also discovered that the engineers I worked for were appalling managers. One, who was a very brilliant man, ordered his work simply by going through his in-tray. If you wrote a report, it might never rise high enough in the pile for him to read it. I used to bribe his clerk, who was called Bashir, to put my reports at the top. This little Indian, in fact, was in charge of co-ordinating all the work. I realized that, unless I learned something about it, I too was likely to be a very poor manager.

Egan was flush with oil money and had a working wife, so the decision to go back to college was perhaps not so brave. After all, it was the middle of the swinging sixties and the idea of unemployment for anyone, let alone qualified engineers, was remote. All the same, the move made Egan a pioneer of business education.

When he graduated from the London Business School, Shell were willing to discuss employment but Egan chose instead to go to General Motors:

> I was offered the chance to work directly for the Treasurer of General Motors UK, which at that time meant all its interests outside Vauxhall Motors. It had four divisions: importing Opel cars, manufacturing and selling Frigidaire products, making AC Delco components and manufacturing Detroit diesel engines.
>
> The treasurer was called Bill de Long, who is currently finance director of Vauxhall, I believe. I had met him as part of a process of persuading companies to hire business school graduates. He was at one of the presentations I made. I was also attracted by the job itself,

which involved pricing and cost estimating and made use of my engineering background as well as taking me into profit planning. I do find numbers pretty easy. I always remember the major figures on our profit and loss account, for example. I wanted to work in a financial environment after business school because money is what it is all about. If you can't talk about business in money terms, you are wasting your time.

He found General Motors was everything he had hoped. He remains deeply impressed with its commonsense financial systems, its five-year cash availability studies and its one-year budgeting systems. The way General Motors did things was, Egan thought, how he expected a well-managed company to operate.

'I also fell in with GM's system of swapping people in and out of finance and general management. I had acquired the notion that I ought to get experience in a number of areas and I wanted to get into general management as early as possible.'

Egan achieved that ambition as head of AC Delco replacement parts operations, which he effectively created as a separate organization. Egan decided it was an area of endeavour which should be much more profitable. It should also merchandize directly to the public, who would demand AC Delco products and pull them through the distribution system. Chief executives-in-waiting never have any inhibitions about saying things and Egan is possibly even readier to shoot his mouth off than most. To his surprise, General Motors agreed with him and gave him the job of proving his hypothesis.

'It was only a little company, with two or three hundred people, but it was a fine experience. It was mostly a training in marketing for me.' He wasn't aware of being precocious. 'I was never conscious of being young. When I moved in to run the replacement parts operation, before it was turned into a separate business, I remember my new boss saying, "John, were you ever young?" I thought it was the most insulting thing. I really felt quite old. I was, I suppose, about twenty-nine.'

He laughs at the memory. He laughs easily and genuinely. 'I don't think I ever took myself awfully seriously. I've always had a lot of fun out of business. But on the other hand I do like to get the job done. I think I've always tried to use a bit of commonsense. That might seem a bit old-fashioned, but generally speaking I don't get dragged away with esoteric ideas. I've always been quite well paid for what I've done, so there has never been a burning ambition to be wealthy. I think I have been far more ambitious for the organizations for which I have worked than for myself, which is probably the right way round.'

His success at AC Delco prompted John Barber's approach. Barber was Lord Stokes's right-hand man, group finance and planning director at what was then a very divisionalized organization called BLMC. Egan accepted because he wanted to work for a British company. He recalls sitting down with a number of Americans at General Motors who he felt talked about their British colleagues as though they were well-trained apes.

He found BL unbelievably different from General Motors. 'General Motors was following basically sensible strategies with relentless energy. BL was following poor strategies with the same determination.' But to start with he thought the battle could be won. 'If the company had remained in divisions, professionalizing those bits of it that needed it, utilizing the fact that each division was supposed to stand on its own feet and disciplining the workforce by closing down factories or companies where they wouldn't work, it might have been all right. But once they began centralizing the basic car-making functions and creating peculiar group organizational structures, I got the feeling that it was going to fail.'

Egan was soon running Jaguar-Rover-Triumph parts and then became sales director of the whole parts division, where he lost no time applying the lessons he had learned at AC Delco. He breathed life into the name Unipart and turned it into a strong brand name and a very efficient, profitable division. In due course he was made managing director of all BL's parts and services operations, which also included some manufacturing and employed about 10,000 people:

> Unipart became a well-managed and extremely profitable organization. I certainly enjoyed running it. On the other hand, by the time I left in 1976 I felt I had done all that I could. By then the 'rescue' by the Government had taken place and the Ryder plan was in force. That was a recipe for total disaster.
>
> I was the service director of BLMC and I could see the enormous changes that had happened to the products. I think it is true to say the quality had gone down. Some very good cars had been replaced by some very bad cars. I felt that the money that Unipart was

47

making was just being thrown away elsewhere in the group. Unipart was a business that any car company anywhere in the world would have been proud to have owned and it was being wasted.

You have to accept it was a failure of management. The men were capable of being efficient and productive. For example, one smallish division of Unipart was SU-Butec, which was a lot of little factories making components where we had very good industrial relations.

One thing that did annoy me was that people thought BL was a uniquely bad British company. In fact it was a typical British company. Looking around at some of our suppliers, I could see that BL was no worse than many. I formed the impression in 1976 that manufacturing on a large scale in a labour-intensive business requiring high quality could not be done in the UK. I thought it was all over. The nation's industry had fallen over the precipice.

In this depressed state of mind Egan left BL to work for another American company, this time Massey-Ferguson. He was attracted by the money, which was a great deal more than he had been earning, and by the job, which was marketing director of its international construction machinery division and co-ordinator of its European operations. Initially he was based in Rome:

It was a busman's holiday. It seemed a nice thing to go and eat some spaghetti and drink some wine. Our children were aged eight and four and thoroughly enjoyed it. My wife learned Italian – she is currently taking a degree at Warwick University in English and Italian literature, which must be a delayed result – but I can't say I did. I was a registered airline passenger most of the time. Massey-Ferguson's construction machines operations were not well run and my recurring advice to the group was to sell them, which they eventually did.

Egan also had a limited period theoretically based in Canada, but again spending most of his time in Europe as corporate parts director. 'I learned that the world was bigger than my home patch. Running identical operations in places as diverse as Italy, Germany, France and the UK was very interesting. Strangely enough, the UK was the best and most cost-effective by the time I had finished with it, which I found extraordinary.'

When Michael Edwardes asked Egan for the second time if he would become chairman of Jaguar early in 1980, it took him several months' hard thinking before he decided to accept, despite his high opinion of Edwardes. 'I was always tremendously impressed by Michael. He was a revolutionary. He was the first man who made it quite clear that the business of management was to manage and that if it wasn't allowed to, the business must be closed down.' But Egan still had limited faith in Edwardes's ability to turn BL round. He was aware that he would be the seventh chairman of Jaguar in six years and that he was taking over a company near to commercial death.

'I took four months to make up my mind,' he told the *Coventry Evening Telegraph* when his appointment was announced in May 1980. 'What really helped was a bunch of kids I saw playing in Banner Lane [Coventry]. I thought: what are those kids going to have if someone doesn't do something about the motor industry? They can't all go on the dole.'

Jaguar Cars originated in the Swallow Sidecar Company, which was founded by Sir William Lyons in 1922 to make motorcycle sidecars. The production of car bodies began five years later and in 1935 the company was floated on the Stock Exchange, which was the first year that the name Jaguar was used. The company name was changed to Jaguar Cars in 1945 and for the next twenty years it earned a world-wide reputation as the maker of high-performance saloon and sports cars, winning the Le Mans Twenty-four-hour Race five times in the 1950s.

Jaguar merged with British Motor Corporation in 1966, as the first step in the creation of what was supposed to become a large integrated motor manufacturing group capable of taking on the rest of the world. For some years Jaguar was protected by Sir William's continued presence, but following his retirement in 1972, its independence was progressively eroded until the company had effectively ceased to exist. Jaguar had become the Large Car Assembly Plant No. 2 of BL, a place where components made elsewhere in BL were put together. The essentials remained those designed and developed by Sir William, but the quality and the commitment to excellence that had been so important an element in Jaguar had disappeared completely.

The effect had been to destroy its reputation, particularly in the United States, which next to Britain was its largest market. Sales had declined from 30,000 cars a year in the early 1970s to under 15,000 in 1979, with American sales slumping from 6,000 to 2,500. Jaguar's reputation for unreliability was the major problem. Jokes were rife about the need to own two Jaguars in order to have enough spare parts to keep one on the road, while American dealers were reputed to try to delay sales until Fridays, so that they would have the weekend to resell the trade-ins they had accepted before irate purchasers returned and demanded their old cars back. Jaguars rusted, rattled and died so badly that their secondhand value was minimal and their image little short of ridiculous.

The fundamental reason was the Ryder plan, which had centralized BL to the point where the difference in quality between its various marques was little more than badge engineering. At the same time, industrial relations were still perilous, in spite of Michael Edwardes's grimly determined onslaught on trades union power, and productivity was at an all-time low.

Egan only accepted Edwardes's offer on condition that he would be empowered to reverse this trend. He did not, at that point, envisage Jaguar as a separate company from BL, but he was determined that it should recover its independence as an operating business.

He arrived with a good deal of sympathy for Jaguar's workforce, which he found in the middle of a pay and regrading dispute. He felt they were justified in being frustrated and disillusioned. His mere arrival acted as a catalyst for change and he immediately began a drive for improved efficiency and reliability.

His initial strategy was simple: to check whether the cars were engineered efficiently, to make sure that they were being built carefully and to discover whether Jaguar's suppliers were meeting the standards that the company needed. The early results were uncomfortable, to say the least. Jaguar drew up a hit list of 150 major faults and, after it had examined the performance of its 1,700 suppliers, concluded that they were responsible for 60% of its quality and reliability problems. Egan's observation that BL was only typical of British industry was reinforced, but he also unearthed deficiencies among foreign suppliers, including ones in West Germany and Japan.

Egan set up what he called 'quality action groups'. Level one problems were dealt with by an area managers' group. Level two problems merited the attention of the group led by David Fielden, a board member and quality director. Egan himself headed the level three group, which took on the major trouble spots and monitored the progress of the other quality groups. He shook the company and the industry by publicizing the failures. Egan's attitude was that Jaguar had nothing to lose in admitting what everyone knew, that its cars had been poor. Only that way, he argued, could the company convince everyone of the need to get better.

His approach to Jaguar's suppliers was brutally direct. If they didn't come up to the standards he wanted, he fired them. There were some very uncomfortable confrontations. 'Our suppliers and ourselves should have common cause to produce parts that are fit for the purposes for which they are designed,' Egan said. 'If the benefits should be fairly spread, so should the pain. Nobody gets a contract from us now unless they agree to this. If they sell us a bad product, they pay for everything; for testing it, for reclaiming it from our factory and for shipping the rubbish back. Out in the field they pay for the replacement part and the dealer's labour.'

The reality was not so draconian in most cases. Egan realized that he needed his suppliers' goodwill and encouraged them to join in task forces to delve into problems. The initial campaign lasted for a year, at the end of which he had drastically cut the rejection rate for major components.

He also tightened up on specifications, raising Jaguar's standards nearer to those of the aircraft industry than the motor trade. It helped lift Jaguar's quality back up to match the reputation of its main German competitors. The cost of improving specifications was heavy, but Egan estimated that it was far outweighed by the saving on warranty claims and the increase in customer and dealer satisfaction levels.

At the same time he launched an almost evangelical crusade within the works to inspire in Jaguar's employees the attitudes towards excellence that they had lost over the previous ten years. He started with regular briefings at management level and then made a series of quarterly information videos which were shown to all the employees in groups of not more than 200, with senior executives on hand to answer questions. One of the videos floated the idea of quality circles and Egan was gratified by employee interest. Within two years, Jaguar had fifty quality circles in its three West Midlands plants.

'Quality circles provide an opportunity for people to influence what they do,' says David Boole, Jaguar's head of public relations. 'Some of the ideas are awful, but there is a surprisingly sophisticated debate. Emphasizing quality does concentrate minds on doing a good job.'

Relations with the workforce were not all sweetness and light, however. For a start, Egan had to reduce Jaguar's workforce by more than 3,000 within eighteen months of taking over. The company was caught up in BL's own continuing financial cliffhanger and its losses, which at one point were running at over £2m a month, had to be eliminated as quickly as possible.

At the same time shop stewards were violently opposed to Egan's plans for shop-floor briefings by Jaguar's foremen. They saw these as undermining their own hold on the men and fragmenting the awesome collective power that the unions still had throughout BL.

The confrontation came to a peak in June 1983, when Egan was already able to boast a miraculous recovery in sales, with Jaguar rolling back the challenge of Mercedes and BMW in the UK and American demand rocketing. The protest took an unusual form: the works did not come to a standstill. Instead, the men refused to listen to ten-minute briefings from their foremen.

It was a last ditch defence by the union leaders. Egan refused to budge:

> We really did not have any good intent from the unions. They would take what they were given and snatch for more. When their productivity was a third of that in Germany, it seemed a rather pathetic exercise. At the end of it all, the only people who still seemed to assume that Britain was an immensely wealthy nation which could afford to have nobody working at all were the unions. If you are going to break out of a vicious circle of despair and failure, the management must take the lead.

In the last six years, Egan has all but succeeded in his crusade to win the hearts and minds of his workforce. He has been helped by Jaguar's incredible recovery. The company is the only one in our sample that has actually rebuilt its workforce back to the levels of 1980. Jaguar once again employs 10,500 people. The big difference is that they are making nearly four cars a year each, compared to less than one and a half six years ago.

By and large, however, they are not the same men. The average age on the production line has fallen sharply, to the early thirties. This is partly due to Jaguar's selective approach to new employees. Egan is a firm believer in education, both on and off the shop floor, and is continually trying to raise the skills of his workers to make them competitive with Jaguar's main rivals. He has created what he calls an 'open learning centre' in the company in which its employees can acquire, in their own time, skills as diverse as micro-computing, welding, English as a foreign language, O-level maths and even engineering to degree level. It is, naturally, enlightened self-interest. 'Overall we are uncompromising in demanding hard work for excellence from Jaguar employees,' Egan says. 'In return, we reward them with performance-related incentive schemes.'

He has been a bitter critic of standards of education in local schools and colleges. He became so annoyed at the poor education he found new apprentices were receiving that he organized a survey of the performance of their teachers: when it was complete, Egan called in the local educational chiefs and told them the survey revealed a sad and sorry state. Teachers were not turning up on time, they were putting on films and leaving the room, they gave no homework, they had no interest in their students' results and their principals didn't even bother to keep the colleges and schools clean. 'They were setting absolutely shocking standards to our apprentices,' he said trenchantly. 'I hated the idea of us doing our best to make our apprentices into top quality workers and not being supported by the outside colleges to which we sent them to learn.' He grins at the memory. 'I must say there has been an improvement since.'

He is a great believer in value for money. He refused to pay any rates in 1981 on the grounds that Jaguar wasn't receiving value for money from the local authority. Coventry had to take him to the High Court to get its money. Confrontation is a natural stance for Egan. People are either for him or against him, and at Jaguar, they are mostly for him. 'I am always asking how far we have succeeded in getting the message through. The answer is probably that if I had today's climate described to me four years ago, I would have settled for it as ideal. I know now we can do much better.'

By comparison with the internal problems of quality and management, rebuilding Jaguar's sales has been relatively easy. Relatively is the operative word. BL had effectively wrecked Jaguar's dealer network by insisting that they took on the whole range of BL cars. There were, for example, 300 dealers in Germany selling the whole BL range from the Mini to the XJS. Now there are thirty dedicated to Jaguar alone selling twice as many cars in total. Many original Jaguar dealers had gone bankrupt or switched to selling Mercedes, BMW, Porsche and other rival cars. Egan sorted through the list and then burst upon the survivors like a firework.

> John believes that what we are about is satisfying customers [Boole says]. He is a salesman. He is really very good at interpreting what the customer wants. He was responsible for instituting a company research programme through which we contact about 10% of our customers by telephone. We can audit the performance of our cars and our dealers very precisely.
>
> John believes that the dealer is half the story. That was something else that was revolutionary. Most of the motor industry in the UK behaved as though it did not want to mix with the people who actually bought the cars. Customers were people who complained. John thinks the opposite. He would ring up a dealer and say: 'Can you lay on an open evening and ask round everyone you can. I'll come up with some of my chaps and give a talk and sell some cars for you.' He made all the senior people at Jaguar go and sell like that.

It was a sharp culture shock to some of Jaguar's top people, as well as to the dealers. Predictably, the American dealers responded fastest. Within a year of Egan's appointment, US sales were rivalling home demand and American dealers were boasting that they could sell 20,000 Jaguars a year if the quality was right and the cars arrived in time for the new year model market. That this was not an empty boast was proved within three years. Jaguar's only problem in the US now is meeting demand – plus the little matter of paying a penalty for using rather a lot of petrol. Egan shrugs. Americans who buy Jaguars can afford petrol.

The astonishing turn-round at Jaguar led inevitably to its flotation as a separate company on the Stock Exchange. It was a spectacularly good deal for BL, which not only sold Jaguar to the public for nearly £300m, but also took £60m out of its subsidiary's booming earnings before the issue in August 1984.

Even so it sold out cheaply. Less than two years later the shares had tripled in value, giving most of the company's employees a profit of £1,500 each on the shares they had been given and potentially making Egan himself more than £500,000. The share issue was eight times oversubscribed, with enormous demand for overseas investors, in particular Americans. About 40% of Jaguar's shares are held in the

US and the company is one of the most highly regarded British stocks on Wall Street.

John Egan has approached the share price in the same way as he approaches the cars themselves. He takes great care to keep UK and US analysts informed of progress and is running a small campaign to educate the investment institutions in the management set-up at Jaguar, so they don't continue to believe that he is essential to its future.

He is not, perhaps, quite as vital as he was. He still works very hard, arriving at work at 8.30 am and not leaving much before 6.30 pm on most days. He does try to keep his weekends free, but he gives up lots of evening to 'eating hot dinners' with business associates. However, he did manage to take time off for his advanced driving test not long ago. 'I was nervous for the first few minutes, but it didn't take long to settle down.' Quite so.

The next challenge that he has to surmount is the production of the new Jaguar, the XJ40, the first the company has ever produced without the driving spirit of Sir William Lyons, who died in February 1985. Something like £200m has been invested in the new car, which is a technological stride forward on which the fortunes of Jaguar will rely for the rest of this century.

It is an incredible statement of the achievement of William Lyons and his engineers that they created a car which we have been able to bring up to date and make as competitive as we have. But the car industry is spanking along at a great pace. There is enormous technical achievement going on all the time in terms of quality, reliability, fuel economy, doing the job the customer wants. The immense improvements in refinement and road holding and so forth over the last few years are really quite startling, even in our own cars, even if they appear to look the same.

Making the new car even better, taking Jaguar another step towards being the best car in the world, is really what John Egan has left to do. He is, of course, quite certain that he will succeed.

The Million Dollar Man

RICHARD V. GIORDANO
Chairman and Chief Executive: The BOC Group plc

Born March 1934
Married – one son, two daughters

Education:
BA, Harvard University
LLB, Columbia University Law School

Business career:
Shearman & Sterling 1959–64
Airco Inc. 1964–78
The BOC Group 1979–
Non-executive director: Grand Metropolitan plc; Georgia
Pacific Corp. (USA); Central Electricity Generating
Board of England and Wales

Richard Giordano is most famous for being by a long way the highest paid chief executive of a British company. For the year to 30 September 1985 his salary was £883,100, which is equal to £17,000 a week. This year the magic million is within his grasp.

Giordano's pay has always been news, ever since it was discovered that he was paid what now seems the modest sum of £271,000 in his first year as chief executive of the BOC Group. Is Mr Giordano worth the expense? asked one newspaper before deciding that he was, as it commented on a fall in BOC's pre-tax profits from £72m to £61m in 1980. Every year since then the subject has been aired: £477,000 for 1981; £579,000 for 1982; down to £529,000 for 1983, after BOC's earnings dipped; up to £771,000 a year later, following a comparable rise in profits; and then the jump to the latest figure, after yet another advance in group profits. Though his salary is not linked directly to profits and with help from the dollar-sterling exchange rate, Dick Giordano was paid £3.5m in five years for leading BOC. Even assuming he paid tax at 50%, that left him with £1.75m – enough to support the Bentley, the Chelsea home, the house in Chappaquiddick, the yacht, the pictures, the fondness for the opera and the cinema, the elegant clothes and the international lifestyle.

You can see why Giordano gets irritated with the media. He shakes his head ruefully. 'Why do the British have this thing about money?' he asks. 'I don't get paid any more than the average American chief executive. I run an international business. Perhaps, if British businessmen were paid more, their companies would do better.'

Giordano didn't even ask for the job. In fact, he was all set to take a year off sailing around the nicer parts of the world after losing an acrimonious battle for control of the company he had been running in the United States. He was quite taken aback when Sir Leslie Smith, then chairman of BOC, persuaded him to become the group's chief executive.

Well, perhaps that is an exaggeration. Giordano is not the kind of man to be easily taken aback. If he was surprised by the offer, he hid it well enough to negotiate the enviable terms of employment for which he suffers such unremitting attention. And he is, after all, a lawyer. How often do you see a lawyer at a loss for words?

It is difficult to imagine Giordano at a loss for anything. He is almost a caricature of the successful American, tall and sun-tanned with a relaxed, egalitarian manner and only a touch of impatience at the corners of his politely smiling mouth. If he had wanted, he could have been a successful politician, a State governor at the least. Not now, though. The exercise of managerial power for more than fifteen years has inevitably eaten into the ability to suffer fools gladly that is essential in one who seeks a mandate from the people.

Dick Giordano first tasted the delights of a top management post at the age of thirty-seven, in 1971, when he was made president and chief operating officer of Airco Inc. He had been with the US industrial gases, plastics and high technology engineering company for eight years, joining in 1963 as assistant secretary after four years with the New York legal firm of Shearman & Sterling. Before that he had taken a law degree at Columbia University, following a BA at Harvard. Just another all-American achiever, in fact. He thinks he was always a leader, even at school, and he always planned to go into industry: 'When I joined the workforce, industry in the United States was the cat's miaow,' he recalls graphically. 'What was good for General Motors was good for the US of A and all that stuff. The prejudices that exist here in Britain have never existed in the United States.'

Giordano earned his business reputation in the early 1970s when Airco was in considerable trouble. It is easy to forget that recession is not a UK phenomenon. The first oil crisis hit the US economy for six and Giordano had to run like crazy to turn his operations round. His style was very active and high profile. He lived and breathed Airco, working all hours, involving all his senior executives in his actions, making his presence felt throughout the group's operations, constantly flying between States stimulating staff and promoting sales. Airco was a sick company and Giordano nursed it back to health with unflagging zeal.

'When I became president of Airco I developed a highly centralized business. 95% of our business was in the United States and it lent itself to that kind of management.' But in 1973 BOC bought a 34% stake in Airco to give the British group a foothold in the US. The next year three BOC directors joined Airco's board and they were very impressed with Giordano's tough approach. BOC decided to increase its holding. To quote the group's brochure celebrating its centenary on 26 January 1986, 'there ensued an international poker game played for very high stakes.' The US Federal Trade Commission began anti-trust proceedings to force BOC to divest itself of its Airco shares. It took BOC three years to have the FTC decision set aside, following which it bid for the whole of Airco's capital. Giordano had just been made chief executive of the American group and fought the offer vigorously, finding another company to outbid the British predator. At the eleventh hour BOC matched the $600m US counter offer and Airco became a fully-owned subsidiary, doubling the group's size.

Dick Giordano was prepared to resign. But not for long. Leslie Smith brought him back to join the board of BOC in January 1979 and a month later he was one of a group of about forty senior executives gathered together in a Cotswolds hotel to discuss long-term strategy. Giordano's forceful arguments in favour of a more dynamic approach to the group made a strong impression. Nine months later he moved to London as chief executive of the whole group instead of Smith, who stayed on as chairman.

There were strong political motives for the appointment. It was a clever way of showing Airco's other valuable executives that their career paths were not blocked by the British takeover. There were practical motives too, because Giordano's only serious rival, BOC's chief operating officer John Williams, had fallen ill.

Compared to a great deal of British industry at the end of the 1970s, BOC was not in bad shape. Its biggest business, the production and sale of gases, is an extraordinary one. Half the world's mass, including the oceans and the atmosphere, is oxygen. Compared to any other commodity, it is superabundant, but the process of extracting it and other gases such as nitrogen and argon is the effective monopoly of a handful of companies, of which BOC is the world's leader.

Before it bought Airco, BOC was already trading in 150 countries. A 1967 corporate advertisement boasted alliteratively: 'You'll find our air separation plants in Auckland, anaesthetic apparatus in Addis Ababa, welding equipment in Warsaw, soda syphons in San Sebastian, cryostats in Cracow, respirators in Riyadh, electrodes in Entebbe, nitrogen in Ndola and oxygen in Ottawa!'

It was – and is – a genuinely international business with factories in fifty countries. Being close to the customers is as important in terms of logistics as it is in terms of confidence in the product. Both, indeed, are fundamental to the group's continuing success. It is a classic example of a company that needs to have an unquestioned reputation for quality and service, which in turn can only be maintained by singleminded devotion to high standards and low costs.

There was nothing wrong with the standards when Giordano took over the reins of power late in 1979, but the singlemindedness had been blurred. Early in the decade the group had decided that its main market offered limited growth. It had already diversified into welding and plunged into a whole range of other activities, from metal trading to frozen pizzas. It was deep into North Sea oil development and was selling time to other companies throughout the UK on the mainframe computer, Britain's biggest, that it had installed in a complex in London's Oxford Street.

But the 1973–4 oil crisis had shaken its confidence and by the time Giordano took over, BOC was already beginning to sell off some of its acquisitions. Giordano inherited a group which was uneasily aware that all was not well. Accepting that things need to be undone is always hard. It must have been a curiously flavoured pill for Leslie Smith to swallow, as he had been the architect of much of BOC's growth in the 1970s. It says a great deal for Smith's personal integrity and his underlying business acumen that he handed over executive power to a recently hostile alien, who used it to reverse many of his own initiatives.

But Leslie Smith was an exceptional businessman himself. He had already created a remarkable board structure for BOC. Smith was a pioneer in developing the role of non-executive directors. He had recruited such surprising people as renegade Labour politician Dick Taverne and academic and writer Michael Shanks to inject new perspectives on the group's business. And to make sure that these outside views were informed, Smith made BOC's non-executive directors devote a considerable amount of their time talking to management and travelling to all parts of the group, preferably in twos and threes so that they could compare notes.

Board meetings were a serious exercise as well. They took two days, with part of the time taken up by board committee meetings – audit and pension policy twice a year and management resources four times – chaired by the part-time directors. The agenda for the board meetings was spent in presenting and discussing the strategic development of the group's main businesses, including an up-to-the-minute survey of prospects for growth, market share, the state of the competition, plans for research and development and investment in plant and management.

In return, he paid his directors handsomely – BOC pays everyone it values well. Smith believed deeply that BOC's non-executive directors had to be strong-minded as well as knowledgeable. He did not want ciphers, but independent voices capable of arraigning the management if it did not measure up to their demands. However, there is a big difference between theory and practice. In spite of the massed intellectual talent on BOC's board, the group was still drifting. It took the arrival of a strong man to put it on a new course and get it moving again.

Giordano had already thought his task through. 'BOC was at a somewhat similar stage in the rest of the world to that which Airco had reached in the States back in the early 1970s. We had businesses that were underperforming. How should we make them better? We had a portfolio that wasn't right. How should we put that right? Compared to Airco ten years earlier, BOC wasn't that sick, but it was clearly overweight. The geographical spread was forbidding and there were cross-cultural differences that were impediments that I didn't have in the US. That took some getting used to.'

Giordano rapidly found out that the high-profile, centralized management style he had used at Airco would not work for BOC. Yet something had to be done to tie the group's far-flung operating companies into a common effort. 'I knew that if the organization remained geographical, we were going to lose a lot of the strategic thrust in any of the businesses that were not world-wide.' But the logistics of BOC's main business made local operating companies essential. And in any case Giordano believed strongly that responsibility should rest as far down the line as possible.

His solution was to change BOC into a product-organized company. 'The product organization was an attempt to break through the geographical barriers, not by centralizing, but by encouraging specialization down product and technology lines. In other words, we have a guy running the gas business who knows gases and talks directly to another guy who knows gases 9,000 miles away. They talk in a kind of technical shorthand. That kind of conversation is bound to be more efficient than one between a guy here talking about gases to a geographical [local] manager with wide product responsibilities.'

The local companies still run their own businesses and the product organization has been laid across the geographical system to create what Giordano likes to call 'networking'. It is not dissimilar to the system that BP has adopted. It can be criticized for giving some people two bosses, their product chief in London and their local boss. Giordano likes that. He's all for his employees learning how to make the right connections to get the resources they want by leaning sideways as well as up or down in the hierarchy.

It took him some time to put this theory into effect. It wasn't until 1983 that a major reorganization on product lines was put through. But he believes it was done with everyone's support. 'I think it was consensus. I mean, there are always one or two holdouts who insist the world is flat, but I don't know of anywhere in BOC where there is anyone saying, let's go back to the old method. There are weaknesses – everything is a trade-off.'

Giordano has spent a lot of time making sure that everyone in BOC knows what he wants. 'We have published a very clear statement of how the company is organized, why it is organized that way, why the name was changed in 1982 to the BOC Group, what our expectations of people are, how we expect them to behave.'

His expectations of behaviour, incidentally, are surprisingly formal. BOC recently moved to new out-of-town headquarters in Surrey, where a former girls' reformatory was transformed into an elegant cross between a greenhouse and an airport terminal, complete with plastic ivy to give that indoors/outdoors feeling. Seduced by the change in atmosphere from downtown Hammersmith to leafy Windlesham, some staff stopped turning up to work in business suits. Giordano jumped on the trend immediately; he may appear relaxed himself, but he is not a believer in his employees suffering the delusion that they are at work to do anything but work. For the same reason, he has discouraged the use of the idyllic parkland surrounding the new head office for any social activity.

No one at BOC should be in any doubt about what the company requires of him. 'We tell 'em and tell 'em again and tell 'em again and tell 'em again.' That sounds a little autocratic, and it is. Giordano's greatest talent is the effective exercise of power. He pays lip service to democracy, but what he practises is an oligarchy. 'Every system has to have checks and balances. If you've got a managerial system that is all leadership – if once the boss says – do it, everyone else falls in line, that is dangerous, because no one corrects his mistakes.' Giordano says the checkers and balancers have to have power of their own:

> I'm not talking about listening to my secretary or the receptionist or the floor sweeper. They don't have power bases. They are not in a position to say: 'Dick, that's dumb.' There have to be people around the organization who, because they have status and staffs of their own, can say: 'Dick, that is not a very good idea because ...' and I must listen. For example, about four or five years ago we had a young planner who was bright, but he was obviously inexperienced and he had no status among the senior management. I went out and hired a fellow who was a senior partner in the Boston Consultancy Group, who came to the company with considerable status, had the pay to go with it, he had my ear, he developed his own expert staff. When he had a view about the business, he spoke with considerable authority. By hiring him, I created a strong independent voice within BOC that I had to listen to.

So did everyone else, of course.

Giordano's only serious rival within BOC is his deputy chairman, Paul Bosonnet, two years his senior and in charge of finance and administration. Bosonnet is to a large extent Giordano's British alter ego. He was made a deputy group managing director in October 1979 at the same time as Giordano was made chief executive and the two work closely together. Like Giordano, Bosonnet is a strategist, and between them they have refined their world view until it is a formidable intellectual model.

In the autumn of 1986 Desmond O'Connell joined the team as group managing director. O'Connell had managed the group's successful growth in health care business since 1980, quadrupling their profits to one-third of the group's total.

Five executive directors, four of them American, currently form an executive committee of the board, which makes the practical decisions, Each operating company is expected to develop a set of goals. Giordano carries around a slim folder containing details of the goals for every

BOC company. He takes out three sheets of paper relating to the goals set one of his managing directors:

> This is a reference point. Every time he and I talk business it ought to be about what's in these pieces of paper. If he's got action he wants to take for which he needs approval, it ought to be on this paper and it should funnel its way up to the executive committee so the other directors can have a crack at it. Checks and balances. Obviously it covers very big, complex activities. There are many other downstream monitoring tools that integrate with this, like the budget. There are a series of budgets submitted by his subordinates about what is going to happen in their businesses in the next twelve months. Obviously the goals have to be consistent with the budget. Then there are our planning activities. I will determine with our planning manager the planning agenda for the year. That has to be consistent with the goals. Research and development have to fit in as well, both central and divisional. So you've got several things all dovetailing. If they don't dovetail, but pass like ships in the night, something's wrong.
>
> It's a goal-setting process at a senior level that is going on between about eight people who are relative peers working with fairly simple documents like this and staying in close communication.

Giordano believes in intensive one-to-one communication with his top people:

> I'm going out on Sunday morning to California to spend a day and half with the fellow who runs our Australian company. We'll spend half a day going through his business plan and talking about his business. I don't bring any staff and neither does he. It's just one-to-one. He knows what he is talking about and hopefully I will understand him. He gets a non-stop flight from Sydney and I get one from London. It's about half way – well, it's a bit further for him because I'm older!

Part of the time will be spent looking back at the performance of the Australian manager's staff – what they did, how well they did it, how good they are, what development steps they require for improvement and, classically, the management succession. One of Giordano's pre-occupations is picking people.

You pick people by looking back at their records first of all, as

65

qualitatively as you can. The quantitative record has loopholes in it – good luck which may not be repeated. The second element I have learned the hard way. Make certain you pick people with a good set of personal qualities. I've picked people who are dishonest and suffered for it. I've had people who were probably intellectually below the salt. I've chosen employees who have been excessively defensive, bordering on dishonesty. They can't stand to see their mistakes in the light of day and have covered them up. I've had people who were just not articulate – brainy and all that, but hell on wheels to communicate with and particularly bad downstream. I've had people who are lazy. There are some people who just don't want to work! [He sounds faintly amazed.] I'm not judging them, but for God's sake don't promote them.

Of course, the riskiest appointments are those from outside the company. But one of the problems is that you are often so anxious to fill jobs that, even from within the company, you close your eyes to something you ought to see. I can't over-emphasize these personal qualities, because the higher you get in an organization, the higher the level of trust required. Trust and co-operation are the cornerstones of this group.

The fact that Dick Giordano does not pay lip service to this statement is reflected in the absence of personal politics in BOC. As a colleague says, 'Dick won't put up with people politics. He craps on it from a great height. There is no one here you have to get onside with. Dick talks to whoever he thinks will be able to help. He generally expects when someone surfaces with an idea, it's been thought through, because that is the way he behaves himself.'

Giordano is relatively kind about failure. He is prepared to accept that it is as much his fault as his appointee's. It is an enlightened view which has been defined by Peter Drucker, the American management guru, who points out that companies do not blame the money they invest in a project that fails to pay off, so they should not blame a man for failing in a job that was beyond his powers.

Giordano can be understanding, but it doesn't stop him being very tough when he needs to. When he arrived at BOC, it had 22,000 UK employees. Now it has 10,000. About a third have gone with businesses that he has sold or closed, but the rest have been cut from businesses that have grown in turnover since.

The success of his management style is reflected in BOC's performance, which is, of course, ultimately reflected in Dick Giordano's pay packet. Under his leadership, BOC has concentrated on the areas in which it is fundamentally strong. His critics can point to this as a negative triumph, but it is one that many competing chief executives would love to be able to boast. 'What a beautiful business to be in!' sighs Christopher Hogg of Courtaulds, comparing the market for oxygen with that for textiles. Equally envious is Peter Walters, as the oil business shudders and creaks.

Everything at BOC seems to be firmly under control. It can even afford to sponsor another Round-the-World Singlehanded sailing race. The current one, which started last August (1986), had twenty-five starters, all dedicated individualists. Giordano, himself a keen yachtsman, admires the qualities required to compete in this race – courage, stamina, technical skills and the ability to distinguish between a gamble and a risk. But, if he ever did sail around the world as a competitor, it would be in another sponsored event, the Whitbread Round-the-World Race for maxi-yachts. They cost hundreds of thousands of pounds, are a logistical nightmare and have huge crews. His crew would be under his absolute command as he drove them compassionately but ruthlessly across the oceans of the world in competition with other dedicated winners. Richard Giordano would love that.

The Man of Property

STANLEY G. GRINSTEAD
Chairman and Group Chief Executive: Grand Metropolitan plc

Born 17 June 1924
Married – two daughters

Education:
Strodes School, Egham
Chartered Accountant

Business career:
Franklin Wild & Co. 1946–57
Maxwell Joseph Group 1957–64
Grand Metropolitan 1964–
Non-executive director: Reed International plc

There is something of Soames Forsyte in Stanley Grinstead Chairman and chief executive of Grand Metropolitan, he has a sense of a deep ethical commitment to commerce. Business, you feel, is to Grinstead almost everything.

To look at he is remarkable for his air of watchfulness, which can be almost menacing. A compact, medium-sized man who carries his sixty-odd years lightly, Grinstead could at one and the same time be what he is – a successful accountant turned businessman – and someone far more dangerous – a gangster, perhaps, or the head of a secret intelligence service. Rather less fancifully, Grinstead is not typical of the chief executives we interviewed. He comes from an earlier generation, which looked on business as an art rather than a craft.

Stanley Grinstead is notoriously uncommunicative to the outside world. He even gives the impression of finding reminiscence an unusual exercise, unlike most top businessmen, who are well used to being quizzed on their careers and on the whole far from averse to recalling them.

'I can't recognize any formative moments when I look back,' Grinstead says after some thought. 'I seem to conform to the pattern that you have identified, in that I was a grammar school boy. When I left school, I remember my headmaster wrote his final report on me, in which he noted that I had decided to become an accountant and that he thought this was something that I would do well. I don't really know how I arrived at that decision, though. One of the reasons was that I regarded accountancy as a very good training ground. It also gave me a very good insight into a variety of businesses. You could spend two or three weeks in a company and then a month in another, and you therefore received a very wide exposure to various aspects of business and commerce. Also you were exposed to top people, so if you had a light it was unlikely it would be concealed under a bushel.'

This perception, however, came later. Grinstead had not been a clerk for long before he was involved in the Second World War. He joined the Navy and became an officer, and then trained in the US as a fighter pilot. The Navy taught him leadership and social awareness. Grinstead is not alone among the New Elite in believing that military training is a positive factor. 'I think it is rather a pity now that young men are not subjected to the experience of having to live together with a degree of equality.' And he recalls being assessed for 'officer-like qualities' and 'going through certain processes to try and develop these characteristics'.

He also saw the world. He spent a year and a half in America and then served in the Mediterranean, India and Australia. He liked the life enormously and nearly made it his career. However, the Admiralty replied to his application for a permanent peacetime job with the offer of a four-year commission plus a tax-free bounty at its end of £5,000. Grinstead was twenty-three and, he told himself, had no commercial value. In four years he would be twenty-seven, with £5,000 and no commercial value. He took the long view and went back to account-ancy.

It was a difficult transition. From the glamorous life of a young ensign he found himself working from nine to six for very low pay. He didn't realize, he says, how unhappy he had been until it was over, but he hurried through his articles in three years. Being unhappy is not, for future chief executives, an excuse for stopping doing something.

For the next five years Grinstead was an audit clerk with Franklin Wild, during a period when most professional firms were happily exploiting their juniors. Before he left, the firm did dangle the prospect of a partnership in front of him, but by then Grinstead had no intention of spending his career in practice.

His motive, he admits, was money. He left the firm without having secured another job. Franklin Wild did its best to discourage its employees from defecting to its clients, but by coincidence, just after Grinstead had left, Maxwell Joseph telephoned the firm, which already acted for the rising property tycoon, to ask if they knew of a qualified accountant who might be interested in a job.

'I had this rather strange interview with Max Joseph. His office at that time was the smallest room in the Washington Hotel, too small to sell as a bedroom, and he shared it with his secretary. She had to

71

leave the room and sit in the hotel lounge while we talked. He didn't really know what he wanted me to do, so he couldn't describe the job or give me any details at all really. It lasted about five minutes during which we talked about nothing relevant, at the end of which he said: "Well, I think you know what I want and, if you'd like the job, you can have it." '

Grinstead knew a little about Joseph through Franklin Wild and the pay was £1,500 a year, which in 1955 was not unreasonable, although not exactly generous. His title was company secretary and his responsibilities were financial and managerial. And vague. 'There was only a small management team. In my side of the organization there was Max and me and about fifteen girls in an office in Clarges St. In the passage of time more people came and a management system burgeoned, but it was very much by necessity.'

Grinstead says it never occurred to him that the company should be investing in management systems or seeking formal training or advice. There was never enough time. 'One was totally committed just keeping all Max's business interests running. I remember not having a holiday for something like two and a half years. Finally I arranged to go away on a Monday. On the Friday I was asked to put it off until Wednesday. When I reached my hotel on Wednesday night there was a telephone message summoning me back to work on Friday.'

Joseph was an inspiring man for whom to work, but was not a strategist. Grinstead says he believes his boss was largely driven by the deal. 'The thing that he always found particularly attractive were assets at a discount. He always believed that an asset could be made to be worth its real value. I think he was prepared to buy anything if it was cheap enough.'

Like many apparently intuitive men, Joseph had an ability to spot good investments that reflected years of experience as well as his special talents. Grinstead says: 'I remember talking to him about hotels. He wanted to buy one and I said: Have you looked it over? He replied: No, but I've driven round it and imagined the worst.' Imagining the worst is a lesson that Grinstead learned thoroughly.

His own responsibilities grew rapidly. The company he joined, only one of Joseph's stable, was sold within eighteen months. Grinstead stayed to run a number of property companies, as well as a hotel company which has become Grand Metropolitan. This was acquired by Joseph in 1957, when its main asset was the Mount Royal Hotel, then making profits of about £225,000 a year. 'We worked at making it worth what Max thought it should be for three or four years, until we had doubled the profits. Then Joseph floated it on the Stock Exchange and promptly merged it with his other hotel company, Grand Hotels Mayfair, to create Grand Metropolitan, so I was redundant again.'

Not redundant in the contemporary sense. Grinstead was at the heart of Joseph's personal empire, a sharp-eyed, agile and steadily growing fish in the increasingly turbulent and shark-infested waters of the 1960s property boom.

Three of the property companies that Grinstead ran in the next couple of years were taken over by the State Building Society, which eventually collapsed in one of the more spectacular scandals to hit the property market. There is always the suspicion that anyone close to the kind of corruption which fraud on a grand scale encourages must themselves be aware of it. Why Joseph dealt with the people at State Building Society, however, was because they were so willing to pay his prices. The fact that they were spending funny money emerged only later. However, Grinstead did not miss any of the lessons that were learned.

Joseph then ran into trouble of his own, when the management he had put in to run Grand Metropolitan after it went public collapsed. Grinstead and Ernest Sharp, who was running Joseph's conglomerate Giltspur and was his other major lieutenant, were asked to divest themselves of half their workloads and come together as joint managing directors of Grand Metropolitan. At that time the profits of Grand Metropolitan were about £1m a year. Today they are £1m a day.

We had a very funny management set-up. There was a large board with, I think, eighteen members at its peak, but we had very few board meetings – at one stage we were down to two a year, for the final and half-year figures. But there was an inner cabinet which comprised Max, Ernest and me. We really ran the company, with a minimum of exchanges with the other members of the board. This went on for years. Joseph, Sharp and I used to meet every week, when we basically discussed possibilities. Because Max had the reputation of being a predator, anything that was for sale was offered to him.

I can't say that we had a strategy. Certainly nothing in writing.

Ernest and I were not similar people, but we had similar backgrounds and a common appreciation of business. Almost without speaking we would agree on a lot of things.

We did have one or two simple tests. We never moved far from our basic activity. We didn't feel comfortable with long order books and we preferred not to be in manufacturing or too far back in the supply chain. We felt very much happier near the consumer, which gives you the opportunity to obtain a close feel for the market and the chance to react rapidly. You don't need to spend lots of money on market research; you've got it all at your fingertips.

It was a management philosophy that was severely tested by Grand Metropolitan's takeover of Watney Mann. By comparison with the mega-mergers of the mid-1980s, the £200m takeover of the brewing company by the up-and-coming hotel group may look small beer, but it was a huge deal when it took place in 1972. It was also widely seen as an amazing piece of cheek, an example of David taking over Goliath. For once the City was right. The takeover was promptly followed by the collapse of the property market and the doubling of interest rates. Grand Metropolitan's borrowings were enormously high, thanks to all its acquisitions; its profits barely covered its interest payments and it was reluctant to sell off assets to reduce its debt because the bottom had fallen out of the property market.

The memory brings a slight smile to Grinstead's lips. 'It was touch and go at some moments. We did have to sell a lot of properties to keep liquid. We had to manage our way out of that problem for a long time.'

It took most of the 1970s before Grand Metropolitan had really digested Watneys. On the plus side was the fact that the brewing group was a treasure chest of undervalued assets. Max Joseph had bought the group because he believed that it was going very cheap. It was only after Grand Metropolitan had won control, however, that the extent of Watneys' assets could be accurately assessed. The new owners found a whole string of hidden or rather forgotten properties: flats overlooking the Thames at Richmond let to elderly boatmen for five shillings a week; empty country cottages waiting to make way for car parks; and of course pubs in prime building sites turning over a few pounds a week squeezed from an impoverished clientele of old age pensioners and the unemployed.

By the end of the 1970s Grand Metropolitan had largely overcome its financial problems and Grinstead raised his eyes from the grindstone to look at the future. The UK did not look at all attractive to him. 'We had a large proportion of our assets, about 95%, and most of our profits here, but the prospects were very dull. There were also political questions and I thought the diversification we needed was geographical. We had looked at Europe – we had, in fact, been there, along with a lot of companies on the back of Britain's entry into the Common Market. We had all spent money there and nearly all of us had come back with our tails between our legs. I'm still – not scarred – but I still have no great enthusiasm for Europe. On the other hand, America did look attractive. I very much wanted to diversify across the Atlantic. Max, however, was not at all keen and he resisted the idea for a long time.'

By 1980 Maxwell Joseph's health was in serious decline and he appointed Stanley Grinstead as deputy chairman. It was a moment of truth which led to Ernest Sharp's resignation. He and Stanley had been working as joint managing directors under Joseph for sixteen years. 'Ernest said we had always been equal and he did not want to be demoted to number two. I think I would probably have done the same.'

Less than two years later Joseph was dead and Grinstead was appointed Chairman and Group Chief Executive of Grand Metropolitan. Now his pent-up desire to expand and diversify was given full rein. In less than five years, Grand Metropolitan has been transformed into a multinational, earning 60% of its profits abroad, of which a third comes from the USA, and has grown to be the UK's tenth largest commercial company, not counting privatized State monopolies like British Telecom. It is hard to overstate Stanley Grinstead's achievement. However reluctant he may be to admit it, he was waiting for his chance to act.

But it is perhaps easy to overstate the degree of change. Compared to companies like ICI or BP, Grand Metropolitan's management structure was and still is ridiculously simple. Where most groups are still struggling to cut their head office staffs from thousands to hundreds, Grinstead sits in his Hanover Square head office with three group managing directors and about thirty executives. 'We've never done anything centrally that could be done out in the field and the fact that we've got nearly 150,000 people hasn't made any difference.' He also believes in close personal control. 'We're always meeting the management. I have to feel really satisfied that the company is in the right area and the chap at the top is competent and that he has a good team around him.' Grinstead additionally imposes very tight financial controls. 'I don't believe in too simplistic a set of criteria. Maybe it's a growing business, or a business in its youth, which you've got to put money into. Or it may be a mature business which ought to be throwing off cash.' If it ought to be 'throwing off cash', pity the poor management which doesn't have a good throwing arm.

He has turned to more formal management systems. The board has been expanded, with Sir John Harvey-Jones, Richard Giordano and Frank Pizzitola, a partner of the American bankers Lazard Freres, as non-executives, and the executive board committee has grown to five, of whom one is American.

The days of the twice-a-year board meetings at a quarter to twelve followed by lunch are also past. 'We even go away for a week each year. We start off with where we were last year and look at whether we have achieved our objectives, whether we were right or wrong. It has been very interesting to see how Grand Met. has evolved from a small company, where I knew everyone and everything, to a size where that's totally out of the question. We've had to move from a very unconventional method of management to something which is much more usual.'

Stanley Grinstead does not have any set of management rules, but his moral pressure on the operating companies to be as efficient and profitable as possible is ever present. He does not believe in management as a precise art, but as a matter of continuous attention to detail:

> I meet each of the group managing directors for half a day a month. We each have an agenda of issues that we want to discuss and we also have a general discussion about factors affecting the business. This helps me keep a feel of what is important. I also have the benefit of being able to see all the group's operations, in a way that he can't, because he is looking after one pocket. There is a lot of interplay and dialogue and personal sessions out of which policies and decisions evolve.

The growth in the last five years has been phenomenal, with sales up from less than £3 billion to £5.5 billion and profits rising proportionately. Stanley Grinstead's mark, however, lies more in the shift in the group's activities into international markets. In 1981, his first full year as chairman, 73% of Grand Metropolitan's sales were in the UK. In 1985, this was down to 57%. At the same time, the spread of activities has widened Grand Metropolitan making a major operator in brewing, food, hotels, wines and spirits, restaurants and clubs, betting shops, health services, petfoods and soft drinks. Its operating companies include Berni Inns, Mecca Bookmakers, Express Foods, Alpo petfoods, Inter-Continental Hotels, Watney Mann, Chef & Brewer, Children's World, Pearle Vision, Forum Hotels, Compass Services, Eden Vale and Ski among others. Its brand names, particularly in beers, wines and spirits, are legion, from Carlsberg lager to Webster's Yorkshire Bitter and from J & B Rare Scotch Whisky to Gilbey's Gin.

As far as Grinstead is concerned the achievements of the past are just the starting point for his company: 'One of my responsibilities is to ensure that the group is flourishing in twenty, thirty years' time and therefore I have to take action and plan for that success. That means not only nurturing and husbanding our existing businesses but also laying down the seeds for future growth.'

He is, of course, anti-regulations. He is convinced that one of the greatest evils besetting the British economy in the last ten years was the Labour Party's prices and incomes policy, under which Grand Metropolitan operated from 1974 until the policy's abolition:

It misdirected a whole generation of management. All you had to do at that point was to go along with the regulatory body and prove to them that your costs had gone up by 10% or 15% or whatever, and then you could put your prices up by the same amount. Good management would have been aware of the need to be efficient and take out redundant plant and so on. But all that was dammed up, costs were allowed to go up, and when the scales were finally torn away we had umpteen years of neglect of our manufacturing base to catch up.

It applied to Grand Met. particularly in brewing. In my judgment it is why beer production is so much lower now. The cost of beer just went up and up and everybody seemed to believe the worm would never turn. For something like thirty years the consumption of beer was on a gently rising trend, but it has come down dramatically in the last few years. In the end the customer rebelled.

Grinstead's personal enthusiasm for public attention is minimal, but he has been forced to the conclusion that a higher profile might have been in Grand Metropolitan's interests, if not his own.

In the last few years Grand Metropolitan has begun to put a small but growing part of its wealth into community services designed to train young people to a level of skills that will help them gain employment in one of a wide range of occupations. So far the rewards of Grand Metropolitan's charitable investment have been less than Grinstead would like, but he has become convinced that education and discipline are essential if Britain's economic future is to be secured. He would not be at all averse to the reintroduction of National Service, preferably geared to providing all young people with marketable skills and to instilling in them the virtues of hard work.

In the absence of adequate training for the new generation, Grinstead's view of Britain's economic future is sombre. But then he has always been a man who has prepared for the worst. Which is why, of course, he has always been pleased with the actual outcome, even if he is careful not to let anyone run away with the idea that even more could not have been achieved.

Grinstead has never been a believer in rhetoric, but he is an outstanding example of what a hard-working pragmatist can achieve. The fact that Grand Metropolitan's growth to one of Britain's largest companies is based on the service and entertainment sectors, where the future is deemed to be brightest, is a measure of Grinstead's deep commitment to providing what the customer wants. As a management philosophy it may lack glamour, but it has the great virtue of working – and that, to the Soames Forsyte in Stanley Grinstead, is the greatest virtue of all.

The Fleet Commander

JOHN HENRY HARVEY-JONES
Chairman: Imperial Chemical Industries plc

Born 16 April 1924
Married – one daughter

Education:
Tormore School, Kent
Royal Naval College, Dartmouth

Business career:
ICI 1956–
Non-executive director: Grand Metropolitan plc

When John Harvey-Jones was selected as chairman of ICI in 1981, it was a surprise to the outside world. He was considered an outsider, a late entrant into the giant chemical group, a maverick with his bright ties and wild hair. For some reason the chairman of the world's fifth largest chemical company is usually described as having piercing eyes. He does have a direct gaze, but no more than most people who are used to asking pertinent questions and receiving answers. Harvey-Jones is a moderately bulky man in his early sixties with a blunt-featured face adorned with a doggy moustache and bushy eyebrows. If there is anything unusual about his eyes, it is probably the speed with which they sort the true from the false.

His appointment was a shock to ICI employees as well, who had become used to the board selecting chairmen unlikely to rock the boat. More than most British companies, ICI had shied away from autocratic leaders, ever since Sir Paul Chambers had disrupted its progress during his reign at the top from 1960 to 1968.

The emergence of a strong leader was made even less likely by the unusually democratic way in which ICI picks its chairman. Election of the chairman, as well as new members of the board, is by secret vote of all the directors. It is not unlike the election of a pope, with discreet lobbying on behalf of contenders and tacit trade-offs between powerful divisional heads. So it was a measure of the crisis ICI felt it was facing that Harvey-Jones was chosen. The magnitude of the task facing him was further reflected in the decision to extend his tenure as chairman from the normal three to five years and to make him 'principal executive officer'. Sir Maurice Hodgson, the outgoing chairman and the man most determined to see his successor empowered to act, couldn't quite get the board to swallow such an overtly dictatorial job description as chief executive, but the fact that Harvey-Jones was going to be more than a moderator was accepted.

That the new chairman was going to go for change in a big way was well known. As organization director, Harvey-Jones had given clear notice of his intentions. 'If you look at our company,' he had told his colleagues brutally in one of his less popular presentations, 'we said in 1970 that we should diversify out of our dependence on petrochemicals. Between 1970 and 1980 we invested nearly £5 billion in new plant. And in 1980, when the shit hit the fan, the company's assets were almost exactly the same percentage both in types of business and geographical area as they had been ten years earlier. As a board we might just as well not have existed.'

When he was elected, hc put his future firmly on the line. 'I am a high-risk choice,' he said. 'What I am going to do may not work out. We failed to read the changing world in the 1970s. If I get it wrong again, I will resign.' And then he got to work. On his first day as chairman he told his fellow directors that they were to report to ICI's guest house in Welwyn for a brainstorming session on the future of the group. One of the first questions he put to them was: should we be in chemicals at all? It was, of course, a rhetorical question. He knew that one of ICI's greatest strengths was its technological base in chemical and allied industries. The other, he saw, was its international spread. ICI sold through wholly owned companies in more countries throughout the world than any of its competitors. The challenge was simply to bring the technology to the markets as profitably as possible.

The first step, predictably, was cost-cutting. Harvey-Jones began at the top, reducing the main board from fourteen to eight. Not everyone who was persuaded to leave had expected that their nominee's crusade would start quite so near home. The ones who were left were equally uprooted, however. Harvey-Jones abandoned the sumptuous board-room with its huge round leather-covered table and its damask walls for all but formal, full-session meetings and transferred his executive team to a small lecture hall with individual desks. Suddenly a mutually congratulatory gathering of the mighty was transformed into a battle briefing of fleet commanders.

The impact has been far-reaching. In the past each of ICI's directors had been responsible for a division, a central function – such as purchasing – and a defined overseas area. Inevitably, they acted as plenipotentiaries to the board for these groupings. Twice a year the chief executive of each division would make a pilgrimage to the imperial headquarters at Millbank, a few hundred yards from the House of Lords, armed with a thirty-five-page submission, plus appendices, itself the tip of an iceberg of staff work, to present to the relevant policy group.

As a system, it was unbelievably bureaucratic. It has been calculated that there could be as many as sixteen intermediaries between a man on the shop floor and the group chairman. It was also inefficient in that most of the main board directors spent their time in committees looking at particular businesses, lacking an overall perspective on the group.

Harvey-Jones's new structure gave two main board directors responsibility for all the divisions of ICI. Three more were put in charge of finance, central planning and research and technology, and two were told to handle overseas affairs. The divisional chief executives discovered they were able to make direct representations to the chairman and his seven-man executive team – if necessary that very week, at the executive board's regular Monday morning meeting, when they might be given twenty minutes to put their case and find themselves with an instant decision.

As well as meeting each week, the board began spending a week a month working as a team on ICI's overall strategy. The rest of the time the executives hurtle around the world looking at ICI's operations and trying to make sure they know what its line management is doing, or trying to do. Harvey-Jones is a great believer in getting real information. He is a dedicated pragmatist. The role of the board, he says, is to take a broad view of future trends, but it cannot do that in an ivory tower.

Having radically changed the role of the board, Harvey-Jones looked distastefully at the enormously long list of staff at the Millbank headquarters and announced that he would like to get rid of the whole place. He hasn't managed to do that yet, but staff cuts have been so large that he has been able to move all the survivors into one building, while the main block formerly used as headquarters is being gutted and transformed into a high-technology communications centre.

When he became chairman, however, the only communications that had been emerging from ICI had been bad news. The declaration of a group loss for the first quarter of 1981, followed by another loss in the second three months, had appalled everyone in ICI, as well as shaking its sternest critics, the City analysts, to the core. This was the first time ICI had ever failed to make money in its fifty-five year history. It was as though two of the Four Horsemen of the Apocalypse had tethered their steeds to the railings at Millbank. Is ICI doomed or can Harvey-Jones save the day? commentators wondered.

In some ways John Harvey-Jones is like a character out of Kipling. He spent the first five years of his life in the Indian princely state of Dhar, about 300 miles north-east of Bombay, where his father was the unofficial chief minister to the Maharajah, an English Count Bronowsky living in semi-regal state. John was the young white Sahib, attended by servants and embraced by the rich, steaming, alien culture of India.

'It was a life of ludicrous luxury by any standards. I don't remember much about it, except my father coming back to England for the 1935 Jubilee and the 1937 Coronation, when I was suddenly hauled out of my prep school and found him and the Maharajah living in Park Lane. A sort of alternating heaven and hell experience.'

Prep school was the hell. Harvey-Jones had been shipped back to board at Tormore School at Deal in Kent, a seaside town not very different in atmosphere from Southsea, where Kipling suffered under the unspeakable Mrs Holloway. 'It was a school of about seventy or eighty middle-class British boys with a very high academic achievement. The thing I loathed about it was the bullying. I was bullied more than anyone else because I was fairly puny and I was different. Until I came to England I'd never seen traffic. I remember arriving in London from the boat train in 1929 and being so terrified that I had to be carried across the road. I found it very difficult to make friends, I loathed the food, it took three months to get a letter from my parents, it was absolutely bloody diabolical.'

Harvey-Jones annoyed his Army family by insisting on going to the Naval training college at Dartmouth. But despite their Indian lifestyle, they were not rich and it must have come as a relief to them that he was able to win a cadetship – more by hard work than academic brilliance, or so he claims. When asked about his education, he always refuses to acknowledge that he was given any. Dartmouth, he says, only trained people: 'In the most ruthless way possible we were taught only those things which it was considered a naval officer needed to know. The aim was to produce a very high standard of retired Lt.-Commander in the belief that the odd Admiral would pop up.' But he does admit to one stroke of luck. As one of the top cadets he was given a last-year cramming in liberal subjects on top of gunnery, engineering and square bashing, and found himself being taught history by the twenty-four-year-old Cyril Northcote Parkinson. 'I think I could still draw you an accurate picture of all Nelson's ships at the Battle of the Nile. Not much practical use, but he knew how to lead. All those discussions with his captains, his "band of brothers", so that when the battle started they all knew what to do.'

Harvey-Jones was fifteen at the start of the Second World War and was soon in action. Indeed, he had what can only be described as an exciting war. He served on two destroyers, the *Ithuriel* and the *Quentin*, which were sunk in the Mediterranean, and then transferred to submarines, partly because he found the noise of heavy guns very painful. 'Moreover, I had an urge to prove myself. There's no question but that the Navy taught leadership as a prime requisite. Submarines taught me that you are all interdependent – anyone in the crew can sink the bloody thing and your respect for each other is generated by your ability to do your part of the job. And moreover submarine crews are very close communities, so if you do something unfair, you hear about it.'

After the war, Harvey-Jones volunteered to learn Russian and found himself living in a Russian mission in Wilhelmshaven dockyard, on the Baltic coast of Germany, acting as liaison officer while the port was officially looted for reparations. Back in London he did a secret job in the Cabinet Office for two years, and was then returned to Germany to run the Navy's stations in Kiel and Hamburg. 'That's when I was given a pot of gold and an old E-boat and told to recruit a German crew. What we were ostensibly doing was fishery protection in the Baltic; you can make your own guesses as to what we were actually doing ... That was tremendous fun. Marvellous, absolutely marvellous!'

That was in 1949, when Harvey-Jones was a self-reliant and unusually adventurous young man of twenty-five. The Admiralty decided to put him back in the proper Navy, where he served as first lieutenant on the *Amethyst* during the Korean War and was then sent off for an Antarctic season with a stay on the Falklands. He returned to join Naval Intelligence, his feet firmly on the path to an Admiral's flag. Instead he resigned from the Navy in 1956 for 'personal reasons'.

He had married a Wren officer and they had had a daughter who, when only four, had contracted polio. Harvey-Jones put his family before a career guaranteed to keep him away for long periods of time. It is easy to underestimate the strength of character this involved. It also reflects another facet which is perhaps more common among British chief executives than is realized: a relative disregard for rewards. Not that the future rewards Harvey-Jones might have been giving up were material ones. His career and the war had hardly given him the chance to acquire a taste for soft living. All his parents' possessions had been destroyed in an air raid and his own had been reduced at one point to his officer's cap and a pair of underpants.

Harvey-Jones applied for a job at ICI because, he says, it was in a basic industry that he could understand. It's as good an explanation as any. Perhaps it was also true that he instinctively gravitated towards another large, institutionalized organization. However ill-equipped an ex-Naval officer may be for industry, he is even less ready to become a self-employed entrepreneur, although it is hard to believe that John Harvey-Jones wouldn't have succeeded at anything he might have put his hand to.

ICI paid him a starting salary of £800 a year, half what he was paid as a Lt.-Commander, and gave him a few weeks' training in work study. Then they sent him to Teesside, to work at the group's huge new Wilton industrial estate on the other side of the river from Billingham. Wilton was an industrial development on a scale previously unknown in the UK. It was a declaration of faith by ICI in a new system of manufacturing chemicals, providing on one site the raw materials, services and space for large-scale expansion in ICI's newest businesses. The site spread over 3,500 acres, including a Victorian mansion called Wilton Castle, and by the time Harvey-Jones arrived in the North East, ICI had invested £57m there, including £15m on a Terylene plant to make synthetic fibres.

The central element of the vast complex's management was the Wilton Council. The Council's members were the representatives of all the ICI divisions involved at Wilton, as well as all the unions, and its chairman had the standing of a divisional director, while one of ICI's main board managing directors was directly responsible for Wilton's affairs. ICI had always taken industrial relations seriously, ever since it was founded in 1926 through the merger of Nobel Industries and Brunner Mond to create a British chemical giant to compete with IG Farbenindustrie of Germany.

Harvey-Jones took to Wilton like a chicken to land. Part of the reason for his immediate success was that he had closed his mind to his Navy experience. 'I started on the assumption that I was a bloody apprentice who didn't know my arse from my elbow.' It was a wise attitude. 'Efficiency in the services is learning the book. Efficiency in industry is looking at a mess, diagnosing a way out, writing an instant book on the problem and, the moment you've finished, tearing it up because the next problem's going to be different.'

Harvey-Jones's very first job was a mess. 'Wilton had an incinerator which was supposed to burn all its waste material, but wasn't coping. It had been decided to build a new one, but this could only be done after an investigation by the Work Study Department. I went down early one morning and I couldn't see the old incinerator, it was hidden under mountains of rubbish. By lunchtime it was quite obvious to me that the real problem was that the chaps weren't putting the right stuff in. They weren't lazing around; there was just no method. The mixtures of waste were wrong, some burnt well, some badly. Put too much in and the thing went out.'

So Harvey-Jones buckled down and worked flat out for three days, after which he handed in his report. The chairman of ICI says he will remember to his dying day his superior looking him up and down – 'I wasn't tottering with fatigue, but I had worked sixteen or seventeen hours a day' – and saying: 'John, you're new in ICI. I'm not going to read this report. Go away and do a proper study and come back in a week's time.'

Harvey-Jones filled in the week helping the men feed the incinerator according to his ideas. When he went back to his boss a week later he handed over his report again and said casually: 'Oh, by the way, we've run out of material to burn.'

It made his reputation at Wilton. His first major achievement, however, was with naphtha. Harvey-Jones was picked to head a three-man mission to find out what the real price of naphtha should be. He spent two days listing every producer in the world who manufactured the chemical and in the next three weeks the team visited them all. It returned to report that the problem was not the price, but the cartel that controlled it. 'The answer', Harvey-Jones said confidently, 'is to refine it ourselves.'

He wasn't the only dynamic manager in ICI in the early 1960s. This time his superior accepted his report and he was promptly given the job of finding ICI partners for a new naphtha refinery, which he managed in two months. The refinery is still operating.

ICI rewarded Harvey-Jones by putting him in charge of selling hydrocarbons, where he immediately distinguished himself by securing the group's first-ever marketing deal over £10m. 'I'd had the good fortune to be in buying, where I'd seen that the sort of contract you can't break is an incremental one where the next 200,000 tons is at a very low price.' The deal was with the Japanese, who offered £10m exactly. Harvey-Jones believed that he should get ICI £10.2m, refused to agree terms, bowed and left. The Japanese finally conceded at Tokyo airport, as he was about to board his flight to London.

By this time Harvey-Jones had a rather awe-inspiring reputation as a troubleshooter. His next task was an internal one. ICI had been trying to introduce an imaginative new employment package which would have produced a career structure for people on the shop floor. It had been hamstrung by a group of shop stewards who had effectively taken control of Wilton. The management response was divided between five operating divisions, none of which was prepared to fight on its own.

The problem had broken several deputy chairmen of Wilton. When Harvey-Jones was given the job, he was welcomed with open arms by the beleaguered managers, who told him they would do anything he wanted. 'No fear,' was Harvey-Jones's reaction. 'It's not my problem. It's ours. We're going to agree what to do and then we're all going to do it together.' He is dismissive about the intellectual success of the exercise. Harvey-Jones is always self-deprecating about his intelligence, although not about his powers of leadership.

From then on his career rise was rapid. By 1970 he was chairman of ICI's petrochemicals and plastics division, as the heavy organic chemicals operation was by then renamed, and on 1 April 1973 he was appointed to the main board. He is both grateful for the speed of his promotion and critical of it. He believes he could have contributed more if he had stayed in some jobs longer. 'If ICI had left me running the petrochemicals division for another two years, it wouldn't have made the slightest difference to my availability for this job. I was trying to achieve a major change in petrochemicals and three years wasn't enough.'

Perhaps there were some people who did not want him to achieve too much; he was a notorious shaker and changer even then. Harvey-

Jones has been used as a troubleshooter for virtually his entire career at ICI and he has loved it. 'If you are a man of only average ability, which I am, go into something bad and you've got a chance of making it better.' He says he was always amazed at the jobs he was given. He used to say to his wife: 'Look what they've asked me to try to do now!' His surprise was a reflection of his belief in his abilities. He always felt capable of improving on the performance of his immediate superior, but was equally certain he couldn't manage the job above that – until he was promoted. He has a theory that his promotion was helped by this attitude, as well as by the fact that he was never career hungry. He may not have been personally ambitious, but he has never been less than outspoken. It is part of his conscious code of moral courage.

Harvey-Jones's willingness to speak his mind was one of his greatest attributes in gaining the support of ICI's unions for hard decisions. No one who presides over a group that has cut its UK numbers by a third in six years can expect to be loved by the workers, but Harvey-Jones had built up a credit for honest speaking and fair dealing with ICI's blue-collar employees that verged on the legendary. All through his career in the group he had applied the lessons he had learned in the Navy about looking after the men under his command, while his patently genuine respect for honest dealing had made his word hard to deny. But he would be deeply disappointed to be seen just as a caring captain of industry. He wants to be remembered as the man who put ICI on a new course to become the best chemical company in the world.

When he became chairman he had already defined ICI's new bearings. It has always had a remarkable record of scientific innovation. Polythene was one of the most far-reaching industrial discoveries of the century. Terylene has been almost as significant for the group. ICI was the first company to produce penicillin by surface culture and Paludrine is still the best-known anti-malaria drug. The beta-blocker Inderal is the second best selling drug in the world and the newer Tenormin is the fastest growing heart drug in the States.

Harvey-Jones has encouraged redoubled emphasis on innovation. 'I'm not a scientist,' he has said, 'but what has really excited me is the growing conviction that we can innovate to order.' A bold claim and one which he sensibly qualifies by saying that the new products have to be marketable. It's all very well having a new protein for plant growth or a defect-free cement, providing enough people want to buy them.

Much greater impact on the shape of ICI has come from his second strategic thrust: giving ICI's customers what they want. Actually, market re-orientation has been the banner under which Harvey-Jones has reshaped ICI most radically. Organic change in a group as huge as ICI would not, he saw, be fast enough. The knife was the only answer. Regardless of cries of lese-majesty, he promptly swapped one of ICI's crown jewels, its polythene business, for BP's PVC operations. Another drastic withdrawal was from manufacture of basic polyester.

To balance these sales and accelerate the shift in ICI's product mix, Harvey-Jones went shopping, buying companies all round the world to improve the product range or the geographical spread, if not both at once. This sounds more dramatic than it was; put against the bulk of ICI the acquisitions do not total a great deal. But they are symbolic of the overriding Harvey-Jones message, which is for ICI to make what its customers want, not make them want what it has.

How successful John Harvey-Jones has been at changing ICI for the better only time will tell. He is not staying on to find out, but firmly resigning at the end of his five-year term, to retire to his Tudor-beamed farmhouse on the Welsh borders. With his donkey cart and his love of nature, he will no doubt enjoy himself as an English country gentleman as much as he has done in both his careers.

CHRISTOPHER ANTHONY HOGG
Chairman: Courtaulds plc

Born 2 August 1936
Married – two daughters

Education:
Marlborough College
MA Hons Classics, Trinity College, Oxford
MBA with High Distinction (Harkness Fellow),
Harvard Business School

Business career:
IMEDE Business School 1962–3
Philip Hill, Higginson Erlangers Ltd 1963–6
Industrial Reorganization Corporation 1966–8
Courtaulds 1968–
Non-executive chairman: Reuters Holdings plc

Christopher Hogg became Chairman of Courtaulds on 1 January 1980. He was eight months off his forty-fourth birthday and had reached the pinnacle of Britain's biggest and best-known textile group just in time to preside over the worst year in its 165-year history.

Just over a year later Hogg reported on the fortunes of his company. Courtaulds' Report and Accounts for the year to 31 March 1981 is one of the classic corporate disaster documents. Printed on drab, thin paper and devoid of pictures or colour, it told a grim story of profits collapsing by £150m to a total loss of £114m, of huge write-offs from asset values and of the wholesale sacking of 20,000 employees, a quarter of Courtaulds' UK workforce. Reporting from the battlefield, Hogg spoke sombrely of the high cost of the year's trading in financial and human terms, and doubtfully about prospects in the UK. But inside he thrilled to the challenge of turning Courtaulds around.

Christopher Anthony Hogg is a decidedly handsome man. He is slim and athletic, his dark hair touched with grey at the temples, his features clean-cut and strong, and he carries his fifty years extraordinarily lightly. There is a touch of asceticism about his appearance, a sense that his relaxed, outgoing manner is a conscious denial of a naturally private personality. He rises determinedly above his innate character, treats all men as equal, wears slightly trendy shirts and signs himself Chris Hogg on all but the most formal occasions.

He is highly admired by the City, which puts him down as first choice to run virtually everything from the clearing banks to British Rail. He has never been short of job offers; they come in all the time. There is something about Hogg that makes him an automatic choice as the man most likely to succeed.

It has always been the case. He is exceptional among our sample of chief executives in going to a major public school, Marlborough

College. When he left in 1954, he had been head of school and a member of both the cricket and rugby teams. He won a Classics scholarship to Trinity College, Oxford, where he obtained a first-class degree. Athlete and scholar, devastatingly good looking, charming, clever and ambitious, he was clearly a young man who had far to go. But he didn't go the way of his peers, who almost to a man made for the City, the media and the professions.

'Looking at it a bit cynically, I think you could say that I had sussed out industry in my Oxford days as an area where the competition was not actually that high. I suspect I thought that instinctively.' But he was also attracted to what he saw as the contribution he could make in industry, not least because another of his characteristics is 'liking to push large stones up hills'. There is a hint of hair shirts about Chris Hogg.

Before going up to Oxford, he had already done his National Service in the Army. It is entirely consistent with Christopher Hogg's destiny that he should have been doing his National Service at the time of Suez. Of course he was commissioned in a crack regiment, though not the Guards. The Paras were more his line: a real elite where a man was measured by his qualities of true grit and officers had to win the respect of their men through leadership rather than rank.

When the Suez crisis came to the boil, Hogg was in Cyprus with the 16th Parachute Brigade. He was already in action, embroiled in a dangerous hunt for EOKA terrorists in the Troodos Mountains, a deceptively mild-looking range of wooded hills in the south-west of Cyprus. The net the Paras were gradually tightening round several terrorist strongholds was abruptly called off late in October 1956. Hogg's battalion, the 3rd, under Colonel Paul Crook, was chosen to drop on Gamil airport, on the outskirts of Port Said. It was the kind of luck most of us would prefer to avoid. The last time British paratroops had experienced a drop under fire had been crossing the Rhine in 1945.

Hogg jumped out of his aircraft shortly after 6 am on the morning of 5 November over Gamil airport. The Paras landed right on top of the defenders. It took them forty-five minutes to overcome all resistance and by 1 pm the Paras began advancing on Port Said itself.

The only way was straight up the road between a lake on one side and the sea on the other. Hogg and his men ran into their first real opposition, a hail of rifle and machine-gun fire from Egyptian troops hidden in reeds marking the edge of a sewage farm. It was like a scene out of a Hollywood war movie, but it was real: the brave British soldiers advancing, Egyptian rockets firing at them from the distance, a Russian-built SU100 gun taken out by a Para with an anti-tank rifle, and Fleet Air Arm fighters strafing the enemy positions. The British troops cleared the reeds and, after spending a scented night near the farm, pushed on to capture Port Said the next day.

Suez has become a music-hall turn in British colonial history, but it had a lasting effect on Hogg: 'I realized very rapidly what it was like to be extremely frightened. You understand a lot about yourself under those circumstances. It's a humbling experience; salutary as well. You learn about other people too: not all bad. It gives you a very positive view of the human spirit and capabilities, but you don't forget your own fallibilities. You don't forget the narrowness of the dividing line between civilized behaviour and bestiality.'

There were other, aspects of Army life which Hogg did not enjoy or find relevant later:

> I think of myself as quite a disciplined man, but I really didn't like the rigidity of the system. I have to admit that for the task the Army is designed for, fighting battles, it is pretty good. One certainly saw that when one got down to the business of risking lives. As an experience it was indispensable in terms of understanding a whole gamut of human emotions and history. But in a diverse, decentralized organization like Courtaulds, there is no way in which you can easily prescribe a set of rules or desired behaviour as you can in the Army. I find that, with exceptions like John Harvey-Jones, military men who come into business are what I call tramlines people. Particularly after the age of thirty-five, they do not find it easy to be creative in a business environment.

When he came out of the Army, Hogg applied for jobs in industry. Among offers was one from ICI which, if he had accepted it, would have made him a direct competitor of Harvey-Jones. Instead Hogg went to Harvard Business School.

> I realized that, although I was as highly educated as the English system could make me, I was hopelessly bereft of knowledge in all sorts of key areas. Harvard was a complete watershed in my life. It transported me into a non-UK environment and gave me an

extremely effective business education, which cut my learning time by two-thirds in areas that I subsequently went into. It was very competitive, but I personally thrived on that.

I was probably preparing myself for a large group. I understand that something like one-third of Harvard graduates either start or end up owning their own businesses. Had I been brought up in an American environment, maybe I would have done that too. I have, however, always taken American attitudes to industrial priorities for granted.

His Harvard qualifications did not help Hogg find a job in British industry. ICI renewed its offer, but showed no signs of valuing his new MBA. 'They offered me an extra £100 a year because I was two years older.' Instead, he used his MBA to get a teaching job in Switzerland at the IMEDE business school, which he used to go around Europe looking at industry. Subsequently he did a three-year stint at Hill Samuel, then called Philip Hill, Higginson Erlangers, in the merchant bank's corporate finance department. He worked first under Sir Derek Palmar, who now heads up Bass, and then under Sir Robert Clark, while Christopher Reeves, now chief executive of Morgan Grenfell, and Cob Stenham, finance director of Unilever, were among his colleagues. Hogg was on the verge of sinking into the rich syrup of the City.

But he has always been a very determined man. When the Industrial Reorganization Corporation was formed in 1966, Hogg was seconded to it. Sir Frank (later Lord) Kearton of Courtaulds was the IRC's chairman. Kearton was a fearsome figure, one of British industry's most dynamic and autocratic people, but Hogg got on just as well with him as with everybody else. At the end of Hogg's two-year term, he went to Courtaulds as a board director of its paints division.

Courtaulds had just doubled the size of its paints division by taking over International Paint, one of the great names in the industry. The group already owned another major paint manufacturer, Pinchin Johnson. Both were old-established companies with worldwide trading empires based, originally, on protecting the hulls and spars of Britain's imperial fleets. Hogg joined the group in December 1968. The following July he was made overseas director and given the job of integrating the two overseas organizations, using his merchant banking experience of mergers.

It is all etched on my memory. The paint industry was low growth and demoralized. International Paint actually missed the profit forecast it had made in the offer document and had to reduce its dividend – the ultimate City sin. It was undoubtedly the toughest job I had ever tackled up to that time and, I think, since. Certainly when I became Chairman of Courtaulds I felt I had been here before, if on a smaller scale. The whole business was a shambles.

Intellectually, it was a gift for the young Hogg. What with his Harvard training and his IMEDE case studies, he had a highly developed faculty for evaluating problems and thinking up strategies. He identified the paint division's strength, which was its worldwide network, and set about turning the company into a professionally run business. Hogg put a rocket under International Paint's research and development team and inspired a drive for technical excellence, which in due course transformed sales and profits.

The way in which science has revolutionized paint in the last twenty years is easy to forget, so much do we take modern products for granted. But International Paint under Hogg was a leader in developing new and better paints, particularly for marine use. Self-cleaning anti-fouling paints, paints to stop steel rusting, paints to use on wet surfaces, quick-drying, high gloss paints, acrylic paints, polyurethane paints, have all come tumbling out to fuel International Paint's marketing successes following the impetus of Hogg's direction.

It took him some time to decide which markets to concentrate on, but he finally settled on selling to industry, especially abroad, where a third of International Paint's sales go to builders and owners of ships. Intensive marketing followed. International Paint records every ship that goes into dock for a refit, for example, and offers to touch up its paintwork. By 1974 the division was making £4m profit and Hogg was a made man.

'International Paint', he says, 'is one of the companies in the UK which I would have thought was a worldwide leader, which it certainly wasn't at the back end of the 1960s. I think I played a significant catalytic role at the start, when it was necessary to have a vision of what might be achieved. If you had asked me in 1975 what I thought I could do, I would have said: build an organization.' But he had had one intimation of mortality:

There was a moment, I think in 1973, when I felt I wasn't going to be able to cope. I suspect it was the cumulative result of exhaustion due to travel and overwork. That was the first time I realized my energies were finite. I recall it precisely because it brought home a lesson taught me at Harvard, not to take decisions when you are tired.

I have relearned the same lessons again and again in my present job. So much of my task has been taking bad news on the chin. That is what is so difficult about turn-around situations. It is so nice to be part of an organization that has a lot of up-and-up to console you for all the hard work and inevitable disappointments. It takes real stamina to keep staring problems in the face.

Which is one of the reasons, incidentally, why Hogg usually cycles to Courtaulds' head office in Hanover Square from his West London home – to keep fit. Another is that he is constantly worried about being too insulated from reality. Being exposed to London's weather and traffic helps him keep his feet on the ground, he says.

In 1975 Courtaulds was on the crest of a breaking wave. Lord Kearton's grand design for the British textile industry seemed to be working. 'Kearton was a great man – one of the major industrial figures in the UK this century. Nobody who was in any degree of proximity to him ever forgot or regretted it.'

Group profits were nearly £120m on sales of more than £1 billion. Courtaulds had increased its UK workforce from 50,000 to 140,000 in under ten years by a huge acquisition programme designed to create a vertically integrated supergroup capable of competing with cheap textiles flooding in from the Third World. And hundreds of millions had been invested in new plant and machinery, much of it in development areas. Courtaulds' drive to rationalize and modernize the UK textile industry was welcomed and supported by both Labour and Tory governments.

But as Hogg became more involved in the textile side of Courtaulds after 1975, as he outgrew the demands of International Paint, he became increasingly worried. The vertical integration was more cosmetic than real. The disciplines he had instilled in the paint division were not apparent in the rest of the group. All Courtaulds had really been doing was stop its UK customers disappearing by taking them over. 'I also think we underrated the extent to which it would be possible for low-cost countries to compete with us, thanks to the sophistication of modern technology. And we did not foresee the strength of sterling due to North Sea oil.'

When Chris Hogg was made chairman, the full extent of the problems staring Courtaulds in the face were still hidden from general view. Profits before tax were up by £4m to £68m, and sales were a record £1.8 billion. But it was all a sham which was stripped away the following year. By then, however, Hogg had already put his action plan into effect:

> I was preoccupied when I became chief executive with the blindness of the management. We had had several years of unsatisfactory results and managers were fearful and lacked confidence. That's a vicious circle. How do you reverse that? You push authority down the line as hard as you can, that's how!
>
> At the same time, I put one single, absolutely clear restriction on everyone. I simply said that every manager had to make a 12% return on capital employed. In cash. Above all, it was a standard by which everyone could succeed, because even a manager who was losing 20% on sales could halve his operation, take out the working capital and there was the cash. He had to worry about what happened next year, but he had succeeded. The cash record of those years was tremendous. I don't know whether Courtaulds would have gone under otherwise, but it was crucial for rebuilding morale.
>
> Along with that went a whole string of decisions, week by week, month by month, that jobs had to be taken out.

Christopher Hogg has a dry, unemotional voice and a reserved expression, but it is a mask. He hated the job losses. They ground away at his finely developed social conscience and his self-esteem, but of course he did not flinch from involving himself in the harsh details.

> I established a pattern for dealing with redundancies, which meant that I knew what was going on in every case. We had a simple set of questions that had to be answered properly before any closure was approved. There were very few big closures. The loss of jobs in the group, over 56,000, was compounded of goodness knows how many individual incidents. I used to have a list in my desk drawer of every announcement of job losses. It ran to about 23 single-spaced typed pages, which totalled upwards of 400 redundancy deals.
>
> The people in the group were extraordinarily conscious of the

need. There was no union resistance in the Fleet Street sense. Most of the textile industry was facing very tough times and understood only too well that what we were up against was production from well beyond our shores.

Ironically, Hogg's most unpleasant experience of closing factories occurred in 1985, long after the worst of the cutbacks had been completed. The long-standing decline in sales of cellulose-based, man-made fibres finally forced Courtaulds to propose the closure of two factories in North Wales, one in Wrexham and the other at Greenfield, only twenty miles away. About 1,100 jobs were on the block, but they were added to a long tally of cutbacks in north-east Wales totalling about 10,000 jobs.

All the same, the Wrexham and Greenfield closures on Deeside might have occurred without attracting widespread attention had it not been for the fact that one week after the public announcement of the two closures on 19 April, the Prime Minister arrived in Deeside on a visit. Margaret Thatcher ran full tilt into a storm of local protest just when she was beginning to feel sensitive about the continuing rise in unemployment. She wrote Hogg a furious letter and a couple of months later he found himself giving evidence before the House of Commons Welsh Committee, which held its enquiry on the spot.

Hogg was given a rough time by the MPs, particularly Keith Raffan, an ex-*Express* journalist who held the local seat of Delyn for the Tories and who had told the Press that he had been prevented from going round the Greenfield factory. This personal attack apart, Hogg was put on the rack over his failure to diversify activities at both factories, allowing their dependence on single products to condemn them to closure. He found it very difficult to take. At times he almost lost his patience. Quizzed on the difference between a profit centre and a cost centre, he replied tactlessly: 'I am not altogether hopeful of being able to get it across to you gentlemen in three minutes.' 'Try!' said Daffyd Wigley, MP for Caernarfon, drily.

Hogg says that in the end Courtaulds did almost exactly what he had planned in the first place. But the enquiry brought him face to face with the personal side of his vast programme of sackings. In five years he had halved the group's labour force and held the unenviable record of firing more people than any company except British Steel and BL, both State owned.

He got rid of them at a remarkably low cost. Courtaulds' average redundancy payment in 1981 and 1982 was £2,500, half the amount paid by ICI, a quarter what British Airways had paid out and a twelfth of what British Steel had given some steelmen to go. Christopher Hogg can fairly lay claim to being the most successful hatchet man in British industry. It is an accolade he hates and he can't wait to win back his reputation as a wealth creator. He has already convinced the City that he is more than just good at cutting Courtaulds' coat to suit its cloth by producing profits that have almost magically managed to be better than the still uncertain industrial background would seem to justify.

But the critics are increasingly inclined to believe Hogg is capable of greater things. One reason is the way he has made Courtaulds' managers go back to school to learn the disciplines he first acquired at Harvard. He persuaded Professor John Stopford to put on the London Business School's first seminar for Courtaulds in 1981, to begin changing the way that the group's managers were thinking and acting. Seminars have continued in various forms ever since, unveiling such business concepts as competitor analysis and the 'experience curve' of low cost manufacturing and its relationship with business portfolios.

Perhaps more important, they have created a cadre of people in Courtaulds with the same approach to business as Hogg. The best measure of the impact of the first seminars is, perhaps, that they had to be suspended in 1983 while more senior managers were sent on a crash version, so that they would stop blocking their subordinates from applying their new knowledge.

Mini-seminars have also been created to spread the new learning through Courtaulds' divisions as quickly as possible as part of the expanding range of courses provided by the group's training centre near Warwick. It has not been as simple as it sounds. Hogg says there are still managers who would like to see the return of autocratic Kearton-style leadership and 'to be told to face East on Thursday mornings, because the world is a cold, hard, difficult place and to have someone who will say which way salvation lies is always seductive.'

What has really made the new learning effective, however, has been Hogg's own commitment to it. He commands such intense respect throughout Courtaulds now that anything with his personal approval carries enormous weight. Belief in his approach has, he hopes, reached critical mass. 'We have gone thirty-five yards out of a hundred. The next thirty-five should be easier, although people are very slow to come to fruition in strategic management. There is no way of shortcutting experience.'

All the same, there are signs that Christopher Hogg believes the worst is over. He sat next to Lord Sieff at a lunch towards the end of 1985, at which the chairman of Marks & Spencer, which is one of Courtauld's most important customers, complimented him gracefully on being the saviour of the British textile industry. It gives Christopher Hogg great pleasure to admit that this is possibly, just true.

The Strategist

TREVOR HOLDSWORTH
Chairman: GKN plc

Born 29 May 1927
Married – three sons

Education:
Hanson Grammar School, Bradford
Chartered Accountant

Business career:
Rawlinson Greaves & Mitchell 1944–52
The Bowater Corporation 1952–63
GKN 1963–
Non-executive director: Thorn-EMI; Midland Bank;
Allied Colloids Group (chairman)

Of all Britain's leading industrialists, Sir Trevor Holdsworth, Chairman of GKN, is possibly the most articulate in his analysis of the problems of British industry and his formulation of their solutions. Encouragingly, he is an optimist. 'If we look back at the record in twenty years' time,' he said confidently, 'the UK recession will be no more than a blip.'

Born on 27 May 1927, Holdsworth has a halo of crinkly brown hair and untidy eyebrows over a pair of thoughtful eyes. Like Sir Keith Joseph, the Tory intellectual whom he resembles, Holdsworth is a strategist. He also believes it is his duty to contribute to the public debate, in his case through a bewildering list of public bodies including the CBI, the BIM, the Engineering Employers' Federation, the Institute of Occupational Health and the Royal Institute of International Affairs, to name but a few. It hardly seems to leave him time to run GKN or to serve, as he has over the years, as a trustee to the Royal Opera House, the Philharmonia Trust, the Ironbridge Gorge Museum and the Anglo-German Foundation for the Study of Industrial Society.

However, the comparison ends there. Where Sir Keith Joseph might be prepared to be martyred in the cause of dogma by the slings and arrows of outrageous fortune, Sir Trevor would first throw himself full length on the ground to avoid being hit and then look round for a way of putting the missiles that fell near him to his own use. But it's unlikely that he would wait around to make himself a target in the first place. 'What I find surprising about the current situation,' he wrote in the *Guardian* in March 1981, 'is that we all seem so surprised by what is happening. What is happening was both inevitable and predictable; only "when" may have been in doubt.'

Holdsworth had seen the recession coming for years. He had read the Brookings Institute report on the state of Britain in 1978 and Sir

106

Nicholas Henderson's much leaked despatch a year later, which also prophesied doom. He had also worked for thirty years in the British steel and engineering industries, in a group that had seen its core business wrenched from it by nationalization and which had spent a decade struggling to rediscover its true identity. To Trevor Holdsworth, the writing was on the wall in letters of fire. In a speech in 1980 he said: 'Today, Germany is 90% more productive than us and France 60%. Put another way, it takes twenty-two million British to do what can be done by only twelve million Germans or sixteen million French. Hence low productivity, low pay, under-employment and now unemployment.'

In Holdsworth's far-sighted view, however, enough is left of our industrial infrastructure to enable the UK to recover. He quotes a foreign industrialist telling him that the British workforce is the best in the world as far as his company is concerned. Neither is he certain that British industry has disappeared quite as extensively as is suggested. GKN's steel works in Cardiff, he says, is now producing over 625,000 tons a year with 500 employees. In 1965 GKN's comparable East Moors works, which was nationalized, employed 4,800 people and never reached that tonnage.

But he is far too canny a Yorkshireman to be more than cautiously optimistic. If there is anything that Trevor Holdsworth believes utterly, it is that the future is generally unpredictable.

Trevor Holdsworth was born and bred in Bradford, the heart of Britain's textile industry, but his abiding impression of industry was gained on a visit by his junior school in the mid-1930s to Walkers & Hall, a steel pressing flatware company in Sheffield. 'That has always lived with me – the sight and sound of metal being processed by hammer and press. Not the textile industry. My impression of that was the cigar smoke coming out of the wool exchange.'

Holdsworth's first ambition was to be a musician. He is well known as a talented pianist, good enough to play the Grieg Piano Concerto as a guest amateur with the Royal Philharmonic Orchestra at a charity concert in the Festival Hall as recently as March 1985. When he was knighted in January 1982, the Bradford *Telegraph and Argus* unearthed details of Holdsworth broadcasting on British Forces Radio and playing the piano for film and TV star Jean Kent during a BAOR tour just after the Second World War. It also fondly recalled him composing songs, one of which, called 'Lonely Me', was broadcast from the old Gaumont

Cinema in Bradford played by its organist, Arnold Loxam.

But the young Holdsworth bowed to the inevitable and his parents, and opted for a much more sensible career – accountancy. 'To be an accountant is a choice of the head, not of the heart,' he told the Institute of Chartered Accountants when it presented him with its Founding Societies' Centenary Award for 1983. 'For almost all of us, to be an accountant is second choice. It lacks the vocational flavour of the doctor or the cleric, the romance of the armed services or even being an engine driver, and the born instinct and natural ability of the artist and musician.'

He is a member of the Institute of Chartered Accountants' new Business Support Group, which is making practising accountants more aware of what industry really involves, and part of Holdsworth's contribution has been to define industry's needs from an accountant's point of view. The first priority, he says, is the generation of resources, the Treasury function. The second is financial systems that give the business the ability to grow and adapt. And the third is management control, which in a sense has to come first. Without accurate and trustworthy information, Holdsworth says, no company can act with confidence.

Holdsworth left school to join local accountants Rawlinson Greaves & Mitchell in 1944, finally qualifying in 1950. For two subsequent years he worked in the firm's Luton office, where he became deeply involved in looking after Laporte Industries, its biggest client. It gave him a valuable education in methods of large companies. 'I knew I was going into industry. I was not going to stay in practice. I didn't like that, too bitty, too disinterested, too remote.'

In 1952 he joined Bowater, the giant UK paper group, as an accountant. He was attracted by the size of Bowater and by the opportunity to manage. 'I remember I was always wanting to change things, find new ways of doing things. Bowaters was really quite primitive in those days. It didn't have budgetry controls, it didn't have management controls, but was run in an old-fashioned style, with what amounted to papermill baronies around the country.'

Holdsworth is a quiet, mild-mannered person and it is hard to imagine that at twenty-five he was abrasive. He was, however, impatient for change. 'I realized that the first thing I had to do was manage my boss. That was the most important thing.' He early recognized that being upwardly mobile should be a painless matter for everyone involved, a belief inspired by the fact that his first superior at Bowater was not the easiest man to work with. Holdsworth is, however, a naturally contemplative person and the step to thinking generally about management skills was not a great one.

His formal introduction to management education came in 1959, when he went to the first course at the Ashridge Management College, along with Patrick Jenkin, amongst others. Holdsworth found it a good experience, but has reservations about embracing too academic an approach to management training. Years later he said, mischievously, that perhaps the best management training course would be one confined to three disciplines: chess, bridge and poker, with the winner collecting the course fees. Holdsworth laughs when he recalls this thrust at the management teaching establishment. 'Chess represents strategic thinking in a wider form, while bridge is working with a partner and poker is taking a calculated risk and having the nerve to see it through. All the elements of business management are captured in these three games.'

Business strategy is his favourite hobby horse. 'People managing businesses tend to get swamped by the internal problems. If you emphasize strategy, you can't ignore the outside world. You have to focus on what your competitors are doing and define your strategy in the light of theirs. It usually enables you to arrive at the few things that are really the lifeblood of the business.' Holdsworth began thinking formally about business strategy after the Ashridge course, which, as an early attempt at business education, was 'a little bit of personnel management, a little marketing, a bit of this and a bit of that' and did not include anything about general management and leadership. He was the first employee of Bowater to have been on a management course: 'I think I suggested it myself, actually.' By then Holdsworth was personal assistant to the finance director, his foot firmly on the management ladder.

When he had joined the group seven years earlier in 1952, however, Bowater was still under the management of Sir Eric Bowater. He was an old-style autocrat who had transformed the company from a paper merchant into a huge manufacturer by persuading Fleet Street's barons, including Beaverbrook and Rothermere, to help finance his new Lancashire mill in 1929. Three years later, Rothermere needed money and sold his shares to Bowater, and Beaverbrook, not wishing to be locked into a large minority holding, also sold out.

One of the group's major investments was a papermill in Tennessee. For a British company to grasp the opportunity to build a papermill in the Southern States when none of the American companies had done so was a very risky and brilliant piece of planning. Holdsworth was lucky enough to be involved. 'I saw how the team to create the enterprise in Tennessee was put together, how the planning was done and how it worked in practice. It showed me how an international project could succeed if you did it on a big enough scale.'

That was in 1955 and Holdsworth spent some time in the States, where he became an early convert to computer power. 'I had the arrogance to say that the whole of the paper mill should really be controlled by computers. I persuaded Bowater to send me for several weeks to Poughkeepsie with IBM. IBM could see that continuous papermaking was an ideal process for computer control. I didn't manage to persuade Bowaters to do it, though.'

He stayed with Bowater until 1963. By then Eric Bowater had died and the whole atmosphere in the company became one of change. Holdsworth was disturbed by the vacuum and was also restless. He was thirty-five and ripe for headhunters Spencer Stuart to poach as deputy chief accountant at GKN, with promotion to group chief accountant a formality upon the imminent promotion of his boss to the board.

His motives for moving were partly the challenge of a new industry and partly the still seductive attraction of a steel engineering company. The reality, of course, turned out to be somewhat different. For a start, Holdsworth found GKN's management systems even more primitive than Bowater's. 'I don't think they had ever thought of themselves as a group until the 1948 Companies Act made them consolidate the accounts.' He was a member of a tiny head office presided over by the chairman, Sir Kenneth Peacock, which was running an extremely decentralized group of companies with virtually no management information. This was surprising, as Peacock was a pioneer of business education. In 1961 he was a founder member of the Savoy Group which, on the basis of a report by Oliver (later Lord) Franks, raised a fund of £10m and created the London and Manchester Business Schools. GKN itself, however, was informal to the point of confusion.

The origins of GKN go back into the sunrise of the industrial revolution. From managing an iron smelting works in South Wales in 1759, John Guest started a family business, which by the end of the nineteenth century was one of the world's greatest iron manufacturers. Arthur Keen began making nuts and bolts in 1853. John Nettlefold set up his company at about the same time, becoming Britain's largest woodscrew producer. The three family companies merged in 1902 as Guest Keen & Nettlefold and expanded throughout the world, initially by providing steel reinforcement and scaffolding to the construction industry and, in the second half of the twentieth century, by supplying the world's mushrooming motor industry.

When it came to management integration, however, the operating companies had shown about as much enthusiasm as Britain did for the Common Market. During the 1960s this changed under the leadership of Raymond (later Lord) Brookes, who set about structuring GKN formally, creating budgets and investment appraisals, setting targets and introducing group policies. Holdsworth's task was to set up the financial systems that made all this effective and to monitor the accuracy of the information that became available.

He was still, in his early days at GKN, no more than a good accountant. By the early 1970s, GKN at least knew where it stood: on very uncertain ground. Steel nationalization had become a real possibility when Labour won the 1964 General Election and it was imposed on a violently obstructive steel industry one year later. This had torn the main rationale out of GKN, leaving a scatter of peripheral companies and a desolate sense of lost purpose. When Labour lost power in 1970, GKN was greatly tempted to revert to being a steel-maker, first by buying back Brymbo and then thinking about the other steelworks. Holdsworth had been involved in these problems during this period, particularly in the negotiations over compensation for the nationalized steelworks.

In 1970 Holdsworth was brought forward from his somewhat insulated position as managing director of GKN Fasteners to face the crucial issues of the day on the group board. It was his first real experience of independent responsibility and one he proved capable of discharging. On his return to the head office he found himself in the centre of the debate about the future of GKN. He was given charge of planning and two years later became a member of what the group called its 'Vice Squad', comprising five vice chairmen, of which Holdsworth was one, responsible for corporate controls and services.

The Vice Squad's first task was to beat out a coherent strategy for GKN. The group had become addicted to planning, including elaborate, five-year forecasts. 'They were really all fiction. I wrote a strategy paper for the board which didn't have a figure in it. Really all we had to decide was a few simple concepts, beginning with the question of whether GKN was a steel group or not. In the end we decided that, no, we were not going to have steel as a central business. We might be a maker of steel because we needed it for a product, but not for itself.'

It was a policy decision with enormous implications for the group. It had only just approved its largest ever investment of more than £50m in a new 600,000-ton steel rod mill. Holdsworth had fought against that, too, ending up a lonely figure on the sixteen-strong board in opposition to the redoubtable Raymond Brookes. It was several years before the collapse of steel demand really made itself incontrovertibly clear, by which time the GKN rod mill had been duplicated by British Steel to compound the overcapacity faced by Ian MacGregor.

The other 'simple concepts' formulated by Holdsworth were equally far-reaching. What, if not steel, he asked, was GKN's business? The main answer was components for the automotive industry. It was a natural change of emphasis, as GKN was already a substantial supplier to the motor industry, but most of its product was, Holdsworth says, of rather primitive, first-stage steel products. The third change in emphasis was to seek international business. Although GKN had reasonably widespread Commonwealth interests, it had no business in the United States, and very little in Europe. But it was already obvious to Holdsworth that the UK motor industry was failing:

The policies of the 1960s had ruined it. How did we as a country manage to destroy what was in 1957 the second largest car manufacturer in the world, when the Japanese didn't really start until 1964? It's a marvellous example of how a country can get it wrong. Whether it was the trades unions or management or the Government doesn't really matter. The Germans were producing up to four and a half million cars a year; the French, the Italians were growing, and we were busy ruining the best part of British industry. But it was quite clear by the early 1970s that there was not much hope for it. So we had to go out to where the industry was – in Europe and America and finally Japan. And that's what we have actually done, piece by piece.

The fourth part of Holdsworth's strategy was to dilute the dependence on the automotive industry and on manufacturing by going into wholesale and industrial distribution, first of steel, metal fasteners and hardware and then of automotive replacement parts. 'It was not wholly successful and we have since sold off the fasteners and hardware businesses. But out of it we have really developed the same kind of dilution in what we now call industrial services. Steel stockholding is not really a wholesale business. Our customers are industry, not the public. We have extended the services concept to cover national pallet pools, industrial waste management and construction industry services.'

Holdsworth was always doubtful about trying to combine different management styles. 'It came over to me very clearly when we bought Firth Cleveland, another Midlands group with a lot of steel engineering interests, but also with a chain of television shops. Of course we said, let's keep them. At the time lots of people wanted to buy the chain, which made us think it must be worth keeping. By the time we realized we were making a mess of it, nobody wanted to buy it. Our instincts said: let's make the shops sell other GKN products, which was totally wrong, but we kept on coming up with new alternatives for this chain. We just didn't understand anything about it.'

Raymond Brookes retired as chairman at the end of 1974 and had already nominated his successor, Sir Barrie Heath, who had joined the board as a non-executive director in 1972.

'Barrie's great strength was that he was motor industry orientated, which was a very good thing for GKN. He was not a strategist. We worked together quite well.' Holdsworth was philosophical and entertained no thoughts of leaving. He was deputy chairman and managing director and continued to work steadily towards the goals he had defined in his, if not everybody else's, mind.

There were times when reaching them must have felt like tickling trout. So near, and yet so far. Engineering was no happier an industrial area to be in during the 1970s than it has been since and, by electing to go into it at the time when most companies couldn't wait to get out, it must be said that GKN was merely fleeing an even worse sector – steel.

But there is a lot to be said for buying when everyone else is selling. You can get some bargains. GKN's biggest was Birfield, a group it picked up in the 1960s, which happened, among a fruit salad of products, to make constant velocity joints for the revolutionary front wheel drive Issigonis Mini. Nobody pretends that GKN foresaw the almost total switch by European and Japanese car manufacturers to front wheel drive, or the extent to which they would turn to the British group for constant velocity joints. But they were quick to exploit the opportunities by investing in new manufacturing plants in Europe and North America. Now America has become a major market for GKN following the oil price crises.

A more intentional achievement has been the group's re-entry into the market for military vehicles. Success in the 1950s at supplying the British Army with troop carriers was followed by twenty lean years awaiting the replacement vehicle. GKN retained a small design and production team to be ready, and in the meantime developed a cheap, tough, wheeled carrier called the Saxon, which it sold around the world. When the UK Ministry of Defence announced its re-equipment needs, GKN won the competitive tender to design, develop and supply the new mechanized combat vehicle called the Warrior.

Even more meritorious, from a management purist's point of view, has been Holdsworth's long-running commitment to using research and development to design products for future markets. The best example of that, hopefully, is GKN's glassfibre leaf spring for vehicles, but that is looking to the future.

In 1977 Holdsworth wrote another paper for the board. This one said bluntly that unless GKN concentrated on completing its evolution into an efficient international group with clearly defined markets, it would inevitably run into a financial crisis in two years' time. 'We were putting things in place. We were setting up a company in Detroit to serve the American auto market; the military market was gradually being worked up. There were a lot of technological things happening, but they were all taking a long time.' Too long, Holdsworth told his colleagues, and argued that one of the reasons was that they were all so involved in running their various pieces of GKN, they were not taking a wide enough view. The board, he said, should run nothing. By the time he became chairman in 1980, he had got the main board's executive numbers down to five.

On 1 January 1980, Trevor Holdsworth was finally appointed chairman of GKN, at the age of fifty-two. As he says, 'Midnight struck, and so did Britain's steel industry.' For the next four and a half months the steel unions were head to head with the BSC chairman, Sir Charles

Villiers. 'It shows that even then we still thought of ourselves as a steel company, in that we assumed the strike was the reason for our problems. We didn't realize that our real trouble was the same as that of the rest of British industry – the recession.'

All the same, GKN was in better shape than most British companies, a frightening number of which disappeared in the next four or five years. Two months before he was appointed chairman, Holdsworth had told the Wolverhampton branch of the British Institute of Management: 'The only thing that is absolutely certain is that almost all attempts at forecasting specific trends and events for the decade ahead will be wrong.' And he quoted, as he frequently does, the poet Robert Bridges: 'True wisdom lies in the masterful administration of the unforeseen.'

In fact, he had foreseen the crash of the 1980s, but that didn't stop him having to hurry forward his strategies at GKN as unceremoniously as did the rest of British industry – the bits that have survived, that is. During 1979 he had been accelerating GKN's sea change at a fearsome pace, making two major acquisitions in the UK, one in France and another two in the US, while selling off its last surviving steel interest in Australia and some of its traditional engineering activities in Britain.

This burst of activity was all part of his 1977 game plan, which had created a chairman's committee, comprising Barrie Heath, the non-executive directors and Holdsworth himself; and a management committee of the executive directors, also including Holdsworth. The result was final acceptance of his plan to move out of British-based engineering and into international motor components supply. It also confirmed Holdsworth as the key man in GKN. His elevation to chairman was, in fact, only a matter of time.

And just in time, as it turned out. In 1980 Holdsworth slimmed GKN's workforce by over 12,000 and saw profits fall from £126m before tax to minus £1m, with the best part of another £100m required for redundancies and plant closures. Prepared as he was, Holdsworth was shaken by the scale of the sacrifices required. The extent to which he had readied GKN to deal with the situation has, however, been shown by its performance since. Six years after that low point in 1980, profits had recovered to £133m and Holdsworth was able to tell shareholders: 'GKN has been transformed from a business with the crude designation of a Midlands metal basher into a world leader in innovation and development of sophisticated new engineering products and in the use of the most advanced technology in design and production ... In any business with as long a history as GKN, there will almost certainly have been a number of periods of reformation and renaissance preceding a new surge forward. I believe that 1980/84 will prove to have been such a period.'

As one would expect of a strategist, Trevor Holdsworth has a sense of history as well as a clear vision of the future.

The Marathon Man

COLIN M. MARSHALL
Chief Executive: British Airways plc

Born 16 November 1933
Married – one daughter

Education:
University College School, Hampstead

Business career:
Orient Steam Navigation Co. 1951–8
Hertz Corporation 1958–64
Avis Inc. 1964–79
Norton Simon Inc. 1979–81
Sears Holdings 1981–83
British Airways 1983–

Some people bring their own luck. When Colin Marshall took over as Chief Executive of British Airways at the beginning of 1983 he found himself in charge of an organization whose morale was in tatters. In some ways it was like the British Army before El Alamein. All its battles had been defeats, its personnel losses had been horrendous, its will to win had been eroded to the point of despair.

The man who had been given the role of British Airways' Montgomery did not look particularly heroic. Colin Marshall has the fine-drawn appearance of a marathon runner whose endless practice to build up stamina has stretched his physique to the limit. It is an apt comparison. If there is anything that singles Colin Marshall out from all the other British chief executives, it is his utter devotion to practising what he preaches to the exclusion of almost everything else. In other respects his appearance is unexceptional. He has a faint resemblance to the late Duke of Windsor; his dress is distinguished only by a lapel badge proclaiming: I fly the World's Favourite Airline; his manner is polite but cool; his smile automatic but rarely deeply amused.

However, he has had an impact on British Airways that has been little short of miraculous. When he arrived, the worst of the job losses were over, and the reorganization of British Airways' fleet and finances was underway. The loss of self-confidence and self-esteem throughout the British flag-carrier was so great that it seemed impossible to many people, both inside the company and out, that it could ever regain its former glory, even if its survival was assured. Marshall found British Airways a by-word for inefficiency, its staff disillusioned and surly, its aircraft dirty and its customers deserting it in droves for its smaller, brighter competitors. He spent nearly six months looking at his new command and then he launched his campaign. For his first battle, he chose the shuttle services to Scotland and the Midlands.

Shuttle was a planners' creation. Economically it was a very good idea, but British Airways' attitude, that the customers had to pay for a walk-on walk-off service by being treated like cattle, was disastrous. When British Midland was finally allowed to compete on the shuttle routes, BA lost a third of its passengers within weeks. Marshall transformed Shuttle. He introduced meals and drinks, he cleaned up the planes and brought in ticket sales and seat allocation before boarding, he inspired the cabin staff into welcoming the passengers with conviction, he chivvied the ground staff so that punctuality improved, and he even taught the pilots how to talk over their intercoms.

The results were dramatic. British Airways clawed back its lost passengers so comprehensively that it wasn't long before its rivals were complaining about unfair trading practices – always a sign of desperation. Colin Marshall had won his first victory.

Its importance was that it underwrote his overall order of battle, which was summed up in a single phrase: Putting People First. 'British Airways' goal is to be the best and most successful airline in the world,' he told his staff. 'This can only be achieved if we deliver a consistently high quality of service to our customers.' And in September 1983 he launched a Customer First training programme which started by putting all BA's 21,000 customer contact staff through a two-day programme on how to make customers feel wanted, which was then extended to everyone else in the airline.

The courses covered subjects like brain functions, control of stress, body language and positive versus negative thinking. They were run by outside consultants, Time Manager International, who had already worked on a similar project for SAS, the Scandinavian airline. To underwrite the importance of the courses, Colin Marshall managed to take part in a large number of them. His motives were simple. The training was telling British Airways staff that the way they treated each other was as important as their handling of customers. Marshall was spreading the message through his own example. 'In an industry like ours, where there are no production lines, people are our most important asset. Everything depends on how they work as a team,' he said at the time.

The seminars produced rapid results. For the first time in the history of the airline, pilots and cabin crew found themselves mingling with check-in operators and baggage handlers. Cabin staff started to tell ground staff what it was like to receive a passenger who had been badly treated at the check-in. Voluntary 'customer first' teams were set up to think of new ideas to improve BA's service and image, like giving single red roses to each passenger on St George's Day, or radically changing the approach to Young Flyers, as the former 'unaccompanied minors' were more positively renamed. New staff were given tickets, pointed at the check-in lines and told to find out what it was like to be on the receiving end.

Gradually, 'putting people first' gathered momentum. Marshall supported it by initiating a complete redesign of the airline's livery, creating a minor controversy by hiring an American design firm, Landor Associates, instead of a British company. He made no apology. Landor, he believed, was the best choice and only the best was good enough. But that did not stop him paying meticulous attention to every detail, even delaying the unveiling of new cabin staff uniforms until he was personally happy about the width of the pinstripes on the stewardesses' suits.

Putting People First was, of course, a rewrite of We Try Harder, which had been the banner under which Colin Marshall had built Avis's international business. What he brought to British Airways was pure Avis, the belief that the customer was first, last and everything and that an airline, like a car rental firm, was only better than its rivals if it gave a better quality of service.

Marshall also brought to his new company a dash of the flair of the International Telephone and Telegram Corporation (ITT), which he learned directly from its chairman Harold Geneen. When he is not touring tirelessly round BA offices and operations throughout the UK and world, Marshall is questioning his senior executives on the performance of their various departments. Every department is regularly summoned to account for itself. It is not a threatening exercise. Marshall is deceptively relaxed, encouraging a round table discussion to which anyone may contribute or be drawn. But woe betide the man who does not know his own facts.

What impresses Marshall's subordinates is his apparently limitless grasp of everybody's business. It is a reflection of his keen intellect and his gluttony for information, as well as his unbelievable capacity for hard work. He is usually at his desk by 7.00 in the morning, by which time he will invariably have looked through the daily papers and rung through to the public affairs duty officer to check on other media comment, and he works at least five and a half days a week, if not seven. Before his first official meeting he often goes walkabout around Heathrow, chatting to baggage handlers and bus drivers as readily as pilots and passengers. When he flies off to any of BA's branches he always makes time to talk to the local staff, however tight his schedule. And that is all on top of his public duties as one of BA's official spokesmen.

There have been times when the load has been nearly too much. At moments of crisis, when British Airways has been involved in unusually tense negotiations with the Government, the Civil Aviation Authority or the unions, Marshall's fatigue has been clearly visible. But he has survived, apparently none the worse for his efforts. He is another who believes that hard work never hurt anyone.

Six months after he took over his new job, he launched what became known as the July Massacre among BA's senior staff. Having studied the management of the group with his customary care, Marshall pulled it mercilessly apart. A large number of senior managers found themselves suddenly pushed out and their places filled by a group of junior managers, many of them well under forty. Hardly any came from outside, but many had been identified by Marshall as likely to respond to the new environment he was about to create. To a quite amazing extent, they have justified his gamble that they would rise to the challenge. They have, of course, become his most ardent supporters.

Marshall's organizational system is very simple. He likes a few high-powered lieutenants who have the main business areas – operations, finance, information management, personnel – under their direct control. He puts complete trust in their ability to run their divisions, although he is completely uninhibited about asking questions of them or anyone else if he wants to know anything. He is always asking questions, about performance, about results, about why the 9.15 shuttle to Glasgow is still on the ground at 9.25 according to the electronic departures screen in his room. It makes him seem omnipresent to many BA employees.

Colin Marshall is not superhuman. He is merely a first-class brain under very careful, rational control, with a power of continuous concentration that is frankly unnerving and an ability to motivate other people that is partly innate and partly the result of his experience stretching right back to his first job.

Marshall went to University College School, Hampstead. It is a day school to which he won a scholarship when he was eleven years old. In those days UCS used to take in a limited number of scholarship boys who were paid for by the local authority. His parents were not rich. His father worked for a company called Daimler Hire, which was principally in the chauffeur-driven car hire business. It was immediately after World War Two, when pupils were not focussed on specific subjects until they had passed School Certificate. Marshall took all the usual subjects, but recalls obtaining his best marks in mathematics. He could easily have won a place and probably another scholarship to university. He left early, however, to go to sea:

> It was an era when this country still had a great seafaring tradition, which had been brought out in my mind by the war. I felt it was a way of seeing the world and also of getting into a form of business. I had established that the Orient Line, the Orient Steam Navigation Company as it was in those days, was taking in cadet pursers. That seemed rather attractive, because I had found out that Orient Line pursers had full responsibility for everything except for actually steering the ship and running the engines.
>
> Unlike some of the shipping companies, in ours the chief steward reported to the purser, who was a very powerful person, with quite a sizeable staff, deputies and senior assistants and cadet pursers. It was something that appealed to me. It was at a time when liners were still the principal means of travel over the longer distances. Air travel was still in its infancy. And the British flag flew over most of the globe.
>
> The navigation side was going to require more formal education and I wasn't terribly anxious to do that. I really did not want to go on into any form of higher education, but to go out and do my thing.

The Orient Line had not been on a recruiting drive to the schools. Nobody did anything like that in those days. Marshall says, 'My guess is that my father mentioned the company to me as one avenue. There were only one or two cadet pursers in every ship, so they were fairly sought-after jobs at the time. I was very pleased to be chosen.' There was no formal training. 'I spent the first eight weeks working in head office, which was in Bishopsgate in the City. I was in the stores department, which was ordering victuals for the ships.' After this brief initiation, Marshall embarked on his maiden voyage in the ss *Orontes*:

> I must say it rubbed off some of the fancier impressions I had had. It happened to be one of the worst times of the year for going down the Red Sea. We sailed through in June with a following wind that was travelling at the same speed as the ship, so we were in still air. All the temperatures, the air, the water and the humidity, were in the high nineties. There was no air conditioning; we hadn't even heard of it in those days in ships; and it was bloody hot. And we were required to wear Mao jackets, done up to the neck, and long trousers, unlike most of the other shipping lines and the Royal Navy, which all moved into open-necked shirts and shorts. I wore three uniforms a day, because they just soaked through.

The *Orontes* carried passengers and Marshall was working with people from his first day aboard. 'People of all nationalities, colours and religions. That was one of the great attractions. I look upon it, frankly, as my university. The university of the world as opposed to studying one specific subject in the midst of some red bricks.' Is there a tiny touch of reverse snobbery in that remark? Perhaps, but one founded in a genuine belief that the experiences he gained were more valuable.

> We had responsibility for the welfare of the crew and the passengers. We had to provide all the entertainment arrangements for the passengers, make sure they were fed and that they knew what they could do at the various ports of call, make all the arrangements for them, get them money when they needed it. And we had to do the same for the crew. It was a hard lesson in many ways, because we were expected to mix with the passengers and contribute to their entertainment outside of our normal working hours, so one wound up working very long days indeed. When we were in port it was not unusual to work twenty-hour days and sometimes right through the night if we had an early departure.

Colin Marshall's almost legendary appetite for hard work had an early foundation.

> We were very short of staff, in spite of the fact that there were plenty of applicants for jobs – I guess the management was reluctant to take on too many people. Although the ships were usually in port

125

for a couple of weeks, we were very lucky if we got more than five days off between voyages. Sometimes, because they were short of crew, we would be switched to another liner and out again within a few days. I remember when I finally left after seven and a half years, I had accumulated over six months' leave due to me.

Most of Marshall's early voyages were between Australia and the UK. In 1954 the company began running cruises out of Australia round the Pacific, as well as trading across the Pacific to the West Coast of the USA and back to England, a voyage that lasted four and a half months. Finally the Orient Line began round-the-world voyages, travelling round the Cape after the Suez Canal was closed. Marshall has memories of ports all round the world: Hawaii, Fiji, New Zealand, Panama, Ceylon, Aden, the Mediterranean ...

He left primarily because he wanted to marry. Being at sea for eleven months of the year was not, he wisely thought, conducive to happy married life, but ambition was the other spur:

> I had become the youngest ever deputy purser in the Orient Line, but my next step to purser was clearly many years away. There were already a dozen pursers for the seven ships and it was a question of waiting for dead men's shoes.
>
> On one leave in Paris for a couple of days, my mother and father were there. One evening we ran into a vice president of Hertz Corporation, whom my father knew. At the end of the conversation, this man said: If you ever want to give up the sea and live in the States, just let me know.

A few months later, when he was planning to marry, Marshall wrote and received a reply offering him a job in Chicago. Marshall's last voyage was his honeymoon, from Southampton to New York on the ss *America*.

He found Hertz very different from the Orient Line: 'I was thrown into middle America, which is much more parochial than any other part of America. In those days it was even more so. I remember my boss saying: "Well, you're all right on a foreign car licence for the first three weeks you are here, but if you go across the State border into Wisconsin, for God's sake don't show them an English licence because they supported Germany in the Second World War and they haven't surrendered yet."'

126

Marshall found American business totally different from anything he had experienced before, but his new colleagues were very welcoming and helpful. He started as a management trainee, working for the vice president in charge of administration at Hertz, who was an extremely intelligent lawyer called Don Petrie. 'He worked very long hours and so, of course, did I. My wife got a job with J. Walter Thompson – she had worked for the advertising agency in London as well. I was there for six months and then I was sent to Toronto to get my feet wet, literally, washing cars and so on, in the front line of the business.' The Marshalls spent the winter in Toronto, which in those days was really like an English provincial city.

The whole place was totally dead after 5.30 in the afternoon. If you wanted to buy a bottle of alcohol of any variety, even of beer, you had to go to the State commission and purchase a permit, which you took to the State liquor shops, of which there were not many. I worked on the rental counters, delivered cars, and for a short time was the manager of one of the small stations in north Toronto. I naturally did the first shift, starting at 7 o'clock, and my first job every morning was to sweep the snow from the front of the office.

And then I guess I got my first real break, when they rang me one day from Chicago and asked if I would become the manager of Hertz's fledgling business in Mexico. Two days later I was on a plane to Mexico City.

The man he was replacing was an elderly American. When Marshall arrived in his office, his first action was to reach into his desk drawer and take out a revolver, which he passed over with the words: 'You'll need this.' Marshall was incredulous. In those days none of the Hertz staff would drive anywhere out of Mexico City without having a gun on the seat beside them, because of the bandits who haunted the highways. The next day Marshall gave the gun to his accountant and told him to sell it and credit the proceeds to Hertz. 'I never had any trouble at all. Some of our staff, admittedly, weren't so lucky. It was a country where life was cheap.'

When Marshall went to Mexico, Hertz had only ninety cars, operating in Mexico City and Acapulco. He ran the business for just over eighteen months, with no Spanish, and by the time he left he had expanded the fleet to nearly 300 cars and had opened branches in

Monterey and Guadalajara as well. 'Those were the two other major cities of Mexico and we knew from customers that there was a demand. As I did many times in my career in the rentacar business, I went to the towns and literally walked the streets, looking for possible locations.'

He was one of the pioneers of the international car rental business and he was left very much on his own, with Hertz judging him almost entirely by results. 'It would not have been the same in the USA. I had a lot of scope. I think in the eighteen months there I saw my boss in Hertz International twice. It was a case of being thrown in at the deep end.'

Marshall learned about starting up new branches and recruiting good staff as he went along. He thinks that there is a lot to be said for making new managers paddle their own canoes even today, depending on the nature of the business. In British Airways, which is interrelated with other airlines, managers need a great deal more understanding of how the operations are run than in a car-hire company with an independent fleet. Business education, in other words, is essential. At Hertz, however, Marshall again failed to receive formal training.

'I was once due to go on a course at Hertz, but my mother-in-law died. The only course that I can ever remember attending was a three-week one in New York for bright managers in ITT subsidiaries. I was the one who went from Avis. I'm not sure I learned very much.'

Marshall considers himself lucky to have been in at the beginning of what became a major world industry. The obvious truth of this obscures the fact that this was true for all his contemporaries as well. Only a very few capitalized on their opportunities to anything like the same extent. Hertz did not miss the potential of their new recruit.

After Mexico Marshall was recalled to Hertz's headquarters, which in the interim had moved to New York. Petrie had by then been named as president elect. It was another example of the luck that seems to accompany talent. He rang Marshall and asked him to work as his assistant. 'I could hardly turn that down. In the meantime, however, my daughter had been born in Mexico City and my wife had become very ill indeed. I had to bring her back to England with the baby and she went to live in her parents' home in Suffolk, where she was in bed for a year.'

By the time Marshall arrived in New York there had been a palace revolution at Hertz and his patron was no longer president elect. He hung about for a couple of months and was then, fortuitously, offered the job of running Hertz in London, partly because of his personal circumstances.

It was another opportunity. When Marshall took over, Hertz had offices in London, Edinburgh and at Prestwick Airport, with 400 vehicles for hire. By 1964, two years later, the number was up to 3,500. At the same time Marshall had opened up Hertz operations from scratch in Belgium and bought an existing business in Holland. From Hertz's point of view, he could hardly be doing better. However, Hertz wasn't the only company to be aware of Marshall's talents.

'In the autumn of 1964 I was in New York, when I was asked to dinner by Don Petrie, who had returned to practising law. He was a great friend of Bob (*Up the Organization*) Townsend, who had been hired to take over Avis, which was a very moribund organization.' To Marshall's surprise, Townsend, now Avis's chairman, was also at dinner that night. 'I found myself engaged in a private conversation in which Townsend asked me if I would take charge of Avis in Europe. It had a series of very independent licensees around Europe. I decided there was plenty of room for another organization.'

Hertz was not pleased. Marshall did not make up his mind until he had talked to his wife. 'It happened to coincide with a point in time when I had proposed to Hertz that they really needed someone running Europe on an overall basis. There were six separate operations all reporting to New York and it was absurd. We never did anything for each other and there was very little attempt at cohesion from the head office. My idea had been turned down the previous week, so I guess I was ripe for picking.'

Hertz carried on with its fragmented management for another two years, by which time Marshall was climbing all over his erstwhile company, eventually taking over first place in the European market for Avis. 'Those were marvellous years,' he recalls fondly.

We started on 1 October 1965 in this country, opening a branch which is still an Avis office just off Marble Arch. It was the first Avis office in the UK. We were represented by Godfrey Davis up until then but we agreed to go our own way and started from nothing.

We opened an office in Glasgow the same day and a week later one in Manchester, with a dozen cars in each place. I don't know what Avis has today, but certainly a few years ago we had over 12,000 cars in the United Kingdom.

Marshall opened up new Avis operations right across Europe at a breakneck pace, as well as sorting out two companies the group already owned in France and Italy which he found to be in a parlous state. He says that he was lucky in recruiting good enthusiastic staff, keen to push Avis forward under the slogan 'We try harder.' It was not just luck:

> They were what I was looking for, so perhaps it was a combination of wisdom and luck. In those days I was looking for local people in each country who had the same level of enthusiasm for the future as I had. A number of them had some experience in the rental business, but others did not. We made some mistakes. If you don't make mistakes you're not trying.
>
> The one particular element in the business was that it involved very long hours. Travel-related service industries have to work round the clock every day of the year. I certainly expected everyone to put in a tremendous effort and they either liked it or they didn't. If they didn't like it, they couldn't stand it, so they did not stay around for very long. But there were very few of those.

Under Marshall's leadership Avis rapidly established itself throughout Western Europe and then expanded into the Middle East, Africa, Australasia and the Far East. That took him, Marshall reveals modestly, just five years, by which time the turnover of the international division of Avis was a third the size of its American operation. The dynamism of the man was almost unbelievable.

'In 1971 I was asked if I would go to New York as Executive Vice-President of Avis, in effect to become Chief Operating Officer. Then I became President in 1975 and Chief Executive at the end of 1976.' Colin Marshall was forty-three. He had been in the car rental business for eighteen years and had climbed to the very top of the American corporate tree, one of the very few Englishmen ever to reach so high. His ability to motivate people into action was held in something close to awe by his subordinates and rivals.

There can be no doubt that he embodies much of what Robert Townsend preaches in his book *Up the Organization*, the sub-title of which, for the record, is: 'How to stop the corporation from stifling people and strangling profits'. In his introduction, Townsend wrote: 'This book is for those who have the courage, the humour and the energy to make a company operate as if people were human.'

Of the way Avis operated, Marshall says: 'We established budgets and we used to make forecasts and have detailed reviews every month of the performance of each of the operations. That is absolutely essential in an international business. You must have financial controls. We knew how the businesses were doing within a couple of weeks of the close of each month and during the months we would receive updates on level of business as well. We put into place a lot of controls which we learned from ITT.'

The supergiant corporation ITT had bought Avis in 1965, a year after Marshall joined. 'ITT was a brilliantly run corporation. I know there has been widespread criticism of Harold Geneen and his management techniques, or maybe not so much his techniques as his personal methods, but I thought he was an outstanding man. I will always look back on the ITT days as very formative from my standpoint.'

Marshall met Geneen infrequently but often enough to have more than a passing acquaintance. His ultimate boss held monthly meetings in New York for the group's American businesses and in Brussels for its international subsidiaries. Marshall occasionally went to the Brussels meetings.

Then in 1971, ITT had signed a consent decree with the US Justice Department to divest itself of a number of businesses in order to avoid violating the country's anti-trust laws. Among the companies put on the 'for sale' list was Avis. But ITT was in no hurry to divest itself of the companies it had acquired. Five years had already passed when Marshall became chief executive, during which Avis had been floated as a public company, but with ITT still holding 45% of its shares, ostensibly at arm's length through the device of a trust. ITT's failure to unload its remaining shares was largely due to the poor state of the New York stock market following the oil crisis, which also hit the car rental business severely. The whole industry suffered badly, particularly in the early 1970s.

Eventually Norton Simon made a takeover offer in 1977. The Avis directors were opposed to the bid. Marshall had been president and chief executive for less than a year and he and his fellow directors preferred an alternative offer from Sears Holdings of the UK, which proposed acting as a white knight by buying 25% of Avis's shares and guaranteeing not to increase its stake. However, the trustee director responsible for the shares still held by ITT refused to abide by the decision of his colleagues to reject the Norton Simon offer.

Instead, he took Avis to court in Connecticut, where the company was registered, and Marshall was roughly handled on the witness stand by the judge, who had originally appointed the trustee. The court ruled against the board and Norton Simon succeeded in its bid, although not before it had been forced to raise its price. 'It was an interesting battle,' Marshall says with masterly understatement.

Some hard things had been said during the fight, but David Mahoney, the boss of Norton Simon, proved generous in victory. Marshall stayed at Avis for two more years, becoming one of two executive vice-presidents of Norton Simon, where he enjoyed learning about the American group's interests in consumer products and food processing. However, the rarefied hierarchy of Norton Simon, the kind of organization which Townsend had so devastatingly mocked, depressed him. Mahoney, he felt, could not make up his mind as to whether Norton Simon was a holding or an operating company and as a result it was neither one thing nor the other.

The companies under Marshall's direction contributed 60% of Norton Simon's sales and profits, but instead of being allowed to get on with managing them, he found himself constantly involved in endless debates about the future of the group.

That phase coincided, as periods of dissatisfaction so often do, with other opportunities. Five companies approached Marshall, three of them British, including Sears, with whom he had kept in touch through occasional dinners with its chief executive, Geoffrey Maitland Smith. Marshall accepted the job of Deputy Chief Executive of Sears Holdings, with the promise of the top job within three years.

For nearly two years Marshall bent his talents to learning about the big British group, finding himself involved in selling businesses and arranging management buyouts among his other activities. But then the head-hunters arrived with an irresistible opportunity. Would he like to become the new Chief Executive of British Airways?

Having spent much of my life dealing with people in travel-related businesses on both sides of the counter, I was clearly suited. I had been a long-time faithful supporter of British Airways and its predecessors. I knew the marketplace, which was very similar to the rentacar business. I felt bad about leaving Sears, but they were extremely gracious. They said it was clearly a great opportunity. I couldn't say no!

The rest is history in the making. The fate of British Airways will always be inextricably bound up with politics, whether it is a public or a private company. In the final analysis, it provides a public service, which is always in conflict with private profit. What should redound to Colin Marshall's eternal credit is his devotion to proving that service must always come first.

The Team Leader

DAVID ARNOLD STUART PLASTOW
Managing Director and Chief Executive: Vickers plc

Born 9 May 1932
Married – one son, one daughter

Education:
Culford School, Bury St Edmunds
Apprentice, Vauxhall Motors

Business career:
Vauxhall Motors Ltd 1950–58
Rolls-Royce Ltd 1958–72
Rolls-Royce Motors Ltd 1972–80
Vickers plc 1980–

David Plastow's commitment to employee communications dates precisely from a dark February afternoon in 1971, only five weeks after he had been given the job of managing director of the car division of Rolls-Royce Ltd, when he had to tell the workforce in the company's major Crewe factory that the indestructible symbol of all that was good and wonderful about British industry was bust. Plastow gave a short, courageous speech, still remembered by older employees, in which he said he was sure that Rolls-Royce had a great future, once it had got its act together again:

> But all I was conscious of was this tinny, impersonal voice coming out of the Tannoy. I didn't have any choice, because that was the only way I could speak to everyone, but I had worked on the shopfloor and I knew we had got it wrong. We had to be able to talk to our people regularly, to keep them informed about what was going on so that things wouldn't hit them without warning.

Rolls-Royce's bankruptcy, of course, was not something that could have been talked about in advance. It was as much a shock to Plastow as anyone, but the principle of keeping his employees as up-to-date as possible is one which he has pursued since then with remarkable determination.

> If a fellow who has been operating a machine in the same place for ten years comes in one Monday morning and finds it has been moved without anyone consulting him, he has every right to be bloody cross. He should have been told three weeks earlier and the chances are he would have been able to suggest an even better place. That makes him committed to the move before it happens.

The word he likes to use is involvement. 'Involvement is not a sophisticated thing. It is a human attitude. Your worker spends more time at his bench than he does at home, yet his wife would not dream of moving the television without consulting him first. Why should we presume we can behave any differently?'

Plastow went to John Garnett at the Industrial Society for his system of worker involvement and came away a convert to Team Briefing. The Industrial Society is Britain's best known independent talking shop on communication between workers and bosses. Keen converts to its teachings carry about a small plastic card which on one side has a list of ten commandments. The first reads: 'Set the task of the team; put it across with enthusiasm and remind people often.' On the other side of the card are three interlocking circles containing the instructions: 'Achieve task; Build team; Develop individuals'.

Team briefing is really just a method of taking information down to the shopfloor by word of mouth. Each team is no more than fifteen people, who are regularly told what is happening in the business, both in their own immediate area and right through the group, by their own supervisor, who then promotes discussions on what has happened and what the company plans to do. The ten rules are full of exhortations to encourage workers to participate, to delegate, to set individual targets, to train and develop, to learn from successes and mistakes, to care for people. Caring is the key word. David Plastow cares intensely about his employees; not in the sense of crying crocodile tears over their plight as underprivileged members of society or being inhibited when it comes to making them redundant – under his leadership Vickers has halved its workforce in the UK to 15,000, of which about 9,000 have lost their jobs and another 6,000 have been sold off with their companies to other groups – but in terms of helping them do ever better, more profitable and therefore more rewarding jobs.

Team briefing became a way of life at Rolls-Royce Motors from 1972 onwards. When David Plastow was appointed Chief Executive of Vickers in 1980, he extended the system right across the group. To begin with, some of his new colleagues did not take it quite seriously enough. Plastow was not amused. He quite frequently attracts the adjective autocratic. He let it be known that it would be 'career-limiting to any member of management who does not support me in the pursuit of this objective'. In spite of this scarcely veiled threat, there were still diehards who dragged their feet. Plastow made an autumn visit to one subsidiary to find that his dictat had not been acted upon. His lips even tighter than usual, he told the director responsible for the business that if the briefing structure was not in place by Christmas, it would be his task to fire the manager in charge, no matter how good he was at other aspects of his job. 'The briefing system is now firmly in place within Vickers,' Plastow reported shortly afterwards in an interview in *Chief Executive* magazine.

David Plastow is exceptional among our sample of chief executives in that he is the only one who served a full five-year apprenticeship on the shop floor. He went to a minor public school at Bury St Edmunds, where he failed his Higher School Certificate. Plastow was unabashed. 'I had a passion about wanting to be a salesman. I had already been on a school trip to Vauxhall Motors' factory in Luton and after failing the exam I went to see the sales director, a great man by my standards, who said: "You don't know what you are talking about. You'd better do an apprenticeship and find out what life's really like." So I thought: Right, you bugger, I will!'

If this sounds like a young man kicking against a conventional middle-class background, the reality is less dramatic. Plastow's father was in the motor trade in East Anglia and his grandfather had been national pennyfarthing racing champion in 1889, so his decision to go to work for Vauxhall was not so much a threat as a promise.

What the hard men on Vauxhall's shop floor made of the eager young man who determinedly mucked in with them, drinking beer, playing in the works rugger team, working just a fraction on the right side of too hard, we will never know. However, the experience made a tremendous impact on Plastow: 'It was enormously valuable, in terms of relationships and understanding what it is all about – and that's folk!'

He was quickly marked for promotion and for the final eighteen months of his apprenticeship Plastow was a sales engineer in Vauxhall's commercial vehicles division, specializing in custom-built bodies for Bedford trucks and vans. He sat in the sales office supporting the field staff for a year and learned in detail how General Motors' business appraisal schemes worked and how its UK subsidiary monitored performance and leadership. He is not sure how much of it stuck. 'It was a very long time ago. I'm sure lots of things have changed since the early 1950s.'

He had not been a fully fledged Vauxhall salesman for more than a couple of years before he was given the job of driving a prototype Vauxhall up to the Scottish motor show to demonstrate to the press. At the show he met the Scottish representative of Rolls-Royce.'I told him he ought to drive a proper car. In return he took me out in a coach-built Rolls and impressed the hell out of me. Then we visited each other's factories and they popped the question.' Which was whether Plastow would join Rolls-Royce Motors as Scotland and North of England sales manager, based in Edinburgh. 'Vauxhall wasn't prepared to make me a field man until I was thirty plus and I was then only twenty-six. General Motors said: "You can't be serious; drinking sherry with people who buy Rolls-Royces isn't proper business." But I thought the chance of getting some experience was worth the risk.'

Plastow got the experience first. The risks came later. He found Rolls-Royce's sales methods rudimentary and began talking to the dealers in the way he had been taught at Vauxhall, hyping them up about customer relations and sales. 'They couldn't understand it. I was the man from Rolls-Royce and I was talking like a General Motors salesman. My chiefs in London couldn't understand it either. It was a very interesting period!' Plastow has a dry sense of humour that takes people by surprise.

> The next thing was to be asked to go to work at the factory in Crewe. I was earning £1,000 a year in Edinburgh and had a Rolls to drive. They offered me an extra £200 and took my car away! It was just before Christmas and the only thing that stopped me writing out my resignation on Christmas Eve was my wife. We had one small child and another on the way and she told me not to be bloody silly!

He was rewarded by being given an ever-increasing range of tasks. Whatever Rolls-Royce thought of Plastow's General Motors' attitudes, it had been quick to notice his application to whatever job came to hand. He was put in charge of manufacturing power plants for the Army and then managed a programme to develop a Wankel diesel for Rolls-Royce's engineering group. 'The only one that ever worked,' Plastow claims.

In 1967 Rolls-Royce's car sales director retired early through ill health and Plastow was offered his job. Four years later he was managing director of the cars' division. He was still only thirty-eight and the world appeared to be his oyster. 'Well, relatively speaking. I didn't see it as a step to the top of the whole group. There was no way that the then culture would have accepted someone from the car business, which was 10% of Rolls-Royce, to run the gas-turbine business, which was 90% of the group.'

Today Rolls-Royce Ltd again boasts an imposing presence. Its marble and glass head office in the West End of London is a high security temple, with aloof uniformed acolytes guarding the holy upper floors. Admittedly more than fifteen years have passed since the Day of Reckoning, but it is hard to believe that the arrogance has recovered its full strength. When Plastow took over as managing director of Rolls-Royce Cars at the beginning of 1971, the group was in the full flush of its image as one of the world's greatest companies – externally, at any rate. But inside the hallowed portals Rolls-Royce was in terminal crisis. Just one month later, on 4 February, Rolls-Royce Ltd finally admitted that it was unable to fulfil its fixed price contract to supply R B211 gas-turbine engines to British and American airlines and called in the liquidators.

Plastow's memories of the next two years are among the most vivid of his life. 'The collapse was a unique experience, a frightening one which I would not like to go through again. I wondered at first whether I had a job at all. I had just started modernizing my house, school fees were coming along, we were buying a colour television set, all the usual things. But at the same time it was fascinating. I remember sitting in a room with Rupert Nicholson, the liquidator, and listening to him talking about the options. He took an amazingly statesmanlike approach, giving us time to make the business acceptable to a buyer and then helping us when we had all sorts of deals on the boil.'

Plastow leaped at the chance offered by Nicholson to hive off Rolls-Royce Motors from the rest of the group and turn it into an independent company. There are parallels with what has happened subsequently to BL and its subsidiaries, like Jaguar and Range Rover, except that no one ever contemplated selling Rolls-Royce to a foreign company! That didn't stop British opportunists making offers. 'Tiny Rowland had a very strong sniff,' Plastow recalls. 'But I always understood that James Hanson put in the top bid, in fact – they were all sealed and we never saw the official numbers – it was high drama, real *High Noon* stuff, with us all sitting in a room waiting to be told who we were going to work for. What happened, however, was that Rothschilds said: "We can do better than Hanson; we'll take Rolls-Royce Motors to the stock market." In due course that is what happened and four days later the market collapsed! It made the decision look a very strange one, but we had got our freedom. It was very exciting.'

David Plastow was managing director of the newly floated company. It was no less than he deserved. Rescuing Rolls-Royce Motors had taken two years out of his life, during which he had worked himself into the ground and nearly destroyed his marriage. By 1974, all that was keeping him going was the adrenalin.

> My judgment was losing its edge. There was no sense of values. The balance had gone out of my life. My relationship with my wife and children had become very brittle. Even more frightening was the discovery that all my senior colleagues had been following my example and had health or emotional problems. I'd never do that again!

One of the results of Plastow's discovery that obsessive overwork is dangerous is a personal memo that each top man at Vickers receives at the end of March every year. In terms that give no room for evasion, the note from the chief executive demands evidence that his lieutenants have taken all their holiday entitlement in the previous year and have put their holiday dates in their diaries for the forthcoming one. And that they have sought the same assurances from the people answerable to them. 'The works have to have their holidays as well, and it is all written up. I work a long day, but I work hard to find time at the weekends. I try to find time for the odd game of golf and to go to the ballet and listen to music occasionally. And not to travel overnight and be sensible at home.'

Very little David Plastow says lacks total conviction, but he has long been notorious as one of industry's worst workaholics. He may have taken the cure, but he is not free of the infection. Secretly, he still believes hard work never hurt anybody and one of the reasons for his company's achievement is the constant pressure on individuals and managers for ever higher rates of productivity.

The second fundamental lesson that the collapse of Rolls-Royce instilled in Plastow was the overriding and all-embracing importance of good communications with the workforce at all levels. The third thing he learned was, predictably, the need to have very, very close control of company finances. He found himself sitting across the corridor from the receiver, who was endlessly asking him for precise financial details before authorizing him to take any action at all.

That year he visited an American company which used what it called a 'flash report' system for monitoring its performance, which meant that the management received preliminary figures from all its operations within three and a half days from the end of each monthly trading period. Plastow was impressed, returned to England, sent his own chief financial man off to the US company for three weeks' training in flash report accounting and promptly installed the method in Rolls-Royce Motors.

Flash reports were a part of Plastow's life, therefore, when he took over at Vickers, to discover that it took that group up to six weeks to find out what had happened each month. That was in 1980, when inflation was raging, foreign exchange rates were gyrating furiously and everybody, including Vickers, was in deep financial trouble.

> If you think about every day of delay in tackling a problem as compounding the problem, because yet more money is going out before you do something about it, the idea of not knowing as soon as absolutely possible how you've done is incredible. By tomorrow I'll have the whole picture worldwide in cash, profits, sales and orders. And we'll be less than one per cent out when the main accounts come out ten days after that. How many companies in the UK can say that?

Perhaps it is time to update Plastow's career to explain the Vickers connection.

Three years after Rolls-Royce Motors had been floated off on the London stock market, profits and sales had risen by 50% and Plastow was looking good. He had been helped by the amazing demand for his cars among rich Americans, to whom prices meant nothing except a chance to reveal how successful they were, but he had also built up the company's diesel engine division until it was producing a quarter of the turnover.

Ever conscious that the luxury car business is at best a vulnerable market area, especially when total output is only about 3,000 vehicles a year, Plastow had been casting round for a related, but independent, business area into which to diversify. At that time diesel engines struck him as a growth business where he could, if he was clever and lucky, build up a genuinely international UK operation. He bought an 18% stake in Britain's other major independent diesel manufacturer,

Gardner, and then put in a bid for truckmaker Fodens to give himself at least one guaranteed end-user.

The takeover bid was commercially logical, but Plastow was also motivated by his desire to grab a demoralized motor company with management problems which he was confident he could solve. Once he had accomplished that, he felt that Fodens would have the right kind of product range to find a place in the international market. His first bid was rejected almost out of hand by Fodens shareholders and his second attempt foundered, predictably, on the rock of the Monopolies and Mergers Commission.

In retrospect, Plastow is probably secretly relieved that he did not have to make good his bold plan. He has become convinced that only major organizations can succeed in the mass vehicle market and has been scathing about the débâcle surrounding the sale of Leyland and Land Rover to General Motors. 'All this pissing about trying to make Leyland British again. It needs desperately to be an international business.' He still thinks that he could have turned the Rolls-Royce diesel business into an international player, but when he eventually found himself thwarted he took the hard decision and sold it to Massey-Ferguson/Perkins, so that it became part of a world-wide group anyway.

In the meantime another opportunity awaited him. He had joined the board of Vickers two years before, in 1975. Vickers was one of Britain's great shipbuilding and aircraft groups, a smokestack dinosaur that was facing the ultimate threat – nationalization of its major business. Two years later the threat became reality and the company nearly died from the shock.

'The whole board was in trauma. It wouldn't do anything. It just said: "We don't know what our compensation will be so we can't invest, we can't act, what would our shareholders say?"' The idea of a merger with Rolls-Royce Motors had actually been floated in 1977, but it was raised again in 1980 with much greater urgency when it became obvious that compensation was not likely to be anything like adequate, in spite of crocodile tears from the Tories. Within twenty-four hours the deal had been agreed in principle, with Plastow pencilled in as managing director.

He inherited thirty-five companies, which added up to about half Vickers' original size and a third of its old profitability, but which, in the absence of the core business, had only a passing relationship to each other. He also took over an organization low on morale and direction. Within days, all that had begun to change.

Plastow's first move was a meeting of the top eighteen senior managers. 'We have to shrink the group before we can grow it again,' he told them. 'Some of you are not going to be here in a year's time.' Next, he installed his beloved flash reporting and brought Vickers' finances under control. 'Then we put a matrix over all the businesses and looked for one key element – the existence of or the potential for international competitiveness. If it wasn't a world player and we couldn't see how it could become one, we sold it.' Plastow sold seventeen companies, one of them Rolls-Royce Diesels, and found that among the remainder he had a property company. '£30m of Vickers' assets were locked up in property which had nothing to do with our business and was earning about 6%, as against 11% from the rest, while I wanted more like 18%. It has taken five years to get rid of all those buildings.' Including, finally, the original Green Giant skyscraper that had so shocked traditionalists when it was erected west of the Houses of Parliament, not a stone's throw from the Tate Gallery.

Since then Plastow has striven unsparingly for the further expansion and development of the still rather disparate bunch of businesses that make up Vickers. He has divided them up into various core areas, but there is very little synergy between them. The idea that a group should contain only related activities has never cut much ice with Plastow. It is the ability to be competitive in world markets that obsesses him.

It is a very simple strategy. We have to make a high quality product and sell it into every market in the world that will take it. There are two issues involved. One is obvious: if you are only selling in your home market, you are vulnerable to one economy or demand for one product. The other is something lots of people don't understand. If you don't compete abroad you don't get the exposure. We've got a little factory in Japan making industrial bearings, we've sold licences for our technology there, we've got people living in Tokyo selling our products. It's tough and we don't make big margins but by God, we're there on the Japanese mainland. We're being exposed to their standards and we know what they are up to – and our competition in the rest of the world is very impressed.

The competition is no less impressed with David Plastow himself. Knighted for services to industry at the beginning of 1986, he still has another ten good, hard-working, team-leading years to look forward to.

The Pinch-Hitter

PETER INGRAM WALTERS
Chairman: The British Petroleum Company plc

Born 11 March 1931
Married – two sons, one daughter

Education:
King Edward's High School, Birmingham
BCom, Birmingham University

Business career:
BP 1954–

The bureaucracy begins at the main reception desk of British Petroleum's triple-tower headquarters on the northern edge of the City of London. A harried receptionist deals with an endless flow of visitors. 'You're going to see whom? Through the swing doors on your right, not the glass doors, and take the lift to the fourth floor. Mr Brown? He's in the South Building across the courtyard. Mr Smedley? I'm sorry, there are so many names. Along to the last lot of lifts and go to the twenty-fifth floor. Sir Peter Walters ... do you have an appointment?'

BP employs around 130,000 people and is the sixth largest company in the world, with sales last year of £40 billion and profits of £3.6 billion. It is by far and away the biggest British company measured in financial terms, and it is extraordinarily important to the UK economy.

Peter Walters is in the chairman's office on the thirty-first floor, a large, traditionally furnished room with a curtained window looking over the Thames. He is in his early fifties, a solidly built six foot, with grey hair brushed straight back and discreetly modern glasses riding on a beak of a nose. His shoulders slope into a slightly pudgy torso and he is dressed in the conventional businessman's suit. He has a rich, engaging laugh and small, soft hands. He has been BP's chairman and chief executive since 1981 and is due to stay in office for ten years, twice the normal term. He was deputy chairman under Sir David Steel for a couple of years before taking over the top job. Steel was a conventional BP chairman, a job usually thought of within the organization as relatively non-executive.

Peter Walters has signally failed to respect this tradition. He has seized control of BP in a way that took a large number of its employees by surprise. Many of them knew remarkably little about him. His personal style was quiet. He had been on the main board for nine years, but he was not expected to get the top job for another five. Most of the employees were also surprised by the extent of the crisis facing BP at the beginning of the 1980s, though they knew there were problems. There had been an air of uncertainty running through the group ever since the first round of oil price rises in 1973. But it is difficult to persuade employees in a giant oil company that their whole future is threatened when high oil prices have lifted turnover to record levels, especially when they are still congratulating themselves on their part in the development of the North Sea and the transformation of their own country into an oil exporter.

Whether they knew it or not, however, BP was in a critical state and Peter Walters was chosen specifically to steer its course away from the rocks. The new chairman had to diagnose very clearly what was going to happen with a flattened oil demand and alarming developments in many areas of natural resources. There was a lack of perspective in BP, which was leaving it with a short-term and essentially backward-looking view of its position.

Walters saw the need to make the businesses owned by BP perform and that the criterion had to be financial. In the 1960s, BP's finances had looked after themselves. The basic management philosophy was linear. This was a highly effective way of ensuring efficient production. Press the button on the management box and it told you how much oil was needed, how to move it across the world to the right refineries to make the correct oil products for each market. If everyone did their jobs, BP had to make money. It was a system based on stable prices, which meant that BP could plan its production ahead, its future profits unrolling in front of it like a red carpet.

All of a sudden, not only did BP not know what the price of oil was going to be in five years' time, it didn't know what it would be next week. This had a profound effect on the organization. BP needed to become able to react to a changing world by taking critical investment decisions. It had to jump from a simple business of cost minimization to being able to guess what would happen if it did this or that, or maybe neither.

The men at the top could no longer rely on a pyramidal management structure, as printed in a diagram in the company manual. They needed to refer to the right people for advice, especially before signing a cheque, and the right people were not necessarily always immediately above. In essence it was a move from a hierarchical to a solar system, with the planets in the shape of the operating companies circling round the central sun. Behold Peter Walters, the Sun King of BP.

Walters's fundamental perception was that the only way to achieve the change he wanted in BP was to make line managers responsible for financial targets – and to drive home their responsibility by making it clear to them that if they met the objectives they agreed, they would be rewarded, but if they failed they would be dismissed. He introduced one other important element. The whole process of change caused the definition of objectives to become much sharper. Peter Walters has forced BP to examine where it is going and what its employees are supposed to be doing more closely than ever before in its seventy-seven-year history.

Walters is not a charismatic leader in the Montgomery mould, in spite of his view of himself as an industrial field marshal. He is not known for his addresses to the troops. He is a persuader, inclined to hesitate until he is sure of his argument but then unsurpassed at making his beliefs those of others. His brain works very fast and he has the ability to go straight to the heart of a subject. He listens to what others have to say, but usually seems to know in advance what that is going to be. He amazes people with what he manages to read and know. It is as though he has antennae out all the time, sucking up information relevant to him. At the same time he appears very relaxed, conveying a feeling of confidence to everyone – and inspiring a touch of awe.

I was selected in the middle of 1981, which happens to be the start of our planning cycle. BP and industry in general were at a pretty low point. Rather like a general taking over a slightly beaten army, I had to clarify BP's objectives. My choices were somewhat arbitrary and personal. Then these had to be communicated. My actions were predicated on my belief in the strong analogies between military and business life, between the role of the general and the role of the chief executive. I see more and more similarities between the two.

I saw it was very obvious what we had to do in terms of cash containment, cash limits on spending – there was nothing we could do about income or the market. We'd got two years to do it. We couldn't just stop everything we were doing – we had the Magnus oilfield which was in a £1bn construction phase – you don't just stop. But, by golly, as soon as we got through the successful Magnus phase we started clawing back on other things.

Then of course the closure of a large number of refinery installations, petrochemical plants, radical swapping out of our weaknesses to other companies. For example, we swapped our North East region oil distribution network. We exchanged our good but too small PVC business – we had just commissioned a new £50m plant at Barry, in South Wales – for the whole of ICI's low-density polyethylene business.

I think any general has to have some catchphrases, at the risk of them becoming platitudes. As I said earlier, communication has to be on a level of constant grinding in, so that people actually remember, even if they laugh at it when they remember. Like Monty and his 'Hit the Hun for Six.'

Part of my message was that there are no sacred cows in BP. It is simple to say, but it released a lot of people's inhibitions about saying, for example: We ought to close Kent refinery but there are 2,000 people there. I'd say: Your job is to worry about the economics, mine is to take a view. You do your job, decide what is right. No sacred cows. It released a lot of thoughts that might otherwise have been bottled up by people who were second-guessing what the chairman had to say.

The other was that BP had always had the idea that unless you were going to be big in a business, then you shouldn't be in it. I said, by my standards, to be big is not a strategy if it is divorced from profitability.

In our coal business, we had said that it was our aim to have twenty-five million tons of produceable coal by 1985. You had to be in the world market place with a figure that people would notice. I said, I don't care whether you are selling one million tons or a hundred million tons, just show me that every step is profitable.

I think the leadership role is important. I've got six managing directors, which is not dissimilar from the structure of BP for the last twenty years, I suppose. But I think even five years ago you would have regarded them as feudal barons representing their parts of the group to the chairman, forcing him to make invidious choices, like the Prime Minister has to do. Right from the beginning of my chairmanship, I made it clear that the managing directors were my representatives to the businesses.

Walters has reinforced this radical change in attitude by labelling

151

everyone down the line of management with responsibility and, as a company board-watcher says, 'tying the labels round their necks. That is something previous chairmen have not done, even though they were sometimes much more domineering.'

Walters exudes the Olympian certainty of the headmaster of a big, successful boys' school. Power sits behind the pleasant smile and he speaks with calm confidence. Here is a man who is certain of himself on every level – well educated, a thinker and a doer, knowing that he has only himself to thank for his achievements, owing nothing to patronage or to inherited privilege or wealth.

He came from what he calls an intelligent working-class background. Of his grandfathers, one was a police constable and the other a school teacher. His father joined the Birmingham City Police force at eighteen and became its youngest chief inspector at thirty-two. Walters himself does not remember any strong feeling of youthful ambition. He passed the Eleven-Plus into one of Birmingham's five King Edward VI grammar schools and then took another exam at twelve to enter King Edward High School. The Birmingham grammar school system was an unabashed intellectual meritocracy comparable to the lycées in France and the best West German schools today. Walters regrets its passing more than somewhat.

'I believe in an elitism based on merit. I can't see how society survives without it. It's part of genetic survival, isn't it? In educational terms, I think we have to educate the fittest to individual and national advantage. I really deprecate the abolition of the grammar schools. I think things have gone downhill ever since.'

He was a very bright boy who actually enjoyed work and learning. He read voraciously without, he says, being a swot. He studied classics at school and passed his A-level equivalents in Greek, Latin, Ancient History and French. He thought of becoming a lawyer and actually enrolled in the faculty of law at Birmingham. His mother was by then a widow – his father had died in the war – and young Walters felt it his filial duty to stay near home. But then the economics of legal training dawned on him. He would, he discovered, be at least twenty-five before he earned any real money as a solicitor or a barrister. Walters decided to go for something more vocational, so he switched within two weeks of the start of his first university term to Commerce.

The choice of both subject and university were crucial, although

Walters did not realize it at the time. Commerce as the title of the degree course, he says, did not reflect what it had to offer:

> Maybe it was a euphemistic way of capturing people who would have been deterred by more accurate descriptions. When I see business school training now, I think, God, I did much of that thirty years ago as an undergraduate. I suppose I was conscious of the quality. I realized we were being taught by some fairly brilliant guys, but at eighteen to twenty-one you don't have many criteria. I welcomed the relevance of the courses, which were a fairly pragmatic mixture of economics, economic history, accounting, finance and industrial psychology. It was a fascinating new world.

Then came National Service. Walters obtained a commission in the Royal Corps of Transport. 'I had a platoon of sixty chaps and I grew up in that time. I found myself handling problems of older men, deserted wives with five children, that sort of thing. Very enlightening for a twenty-year-old.'

He stayed in Britain and passed out of his officer training course as senior under-officer and best cadet, which entitled him, so he thought, to the pick of the postings. 'From my group there was only one overseas posting – in Singapore. I chose it but I didn't get it. It went to the general's son who came near the bottom of the passing-out list. I went to HQ, Western Command, Chester.'

Peter Walters says the training he received as an officer cadet and the opportunity to practise it as a young officer have had a profound impact on his style and his life. It made him realize the need for observation, for good communications and for telling people about objectives. 'In the Army there are some quite humble people to whom you have to describe things in terms they can understand. You have to give them objectives that stand the shocks of combat. You can't be too clever, or when you've knocked off one objective your men won't remember what the next one is.'

He also learned a lot about report writing. 'You are actually taught to write reports in the Army: information, intention, method, administration, communication. Then you have to go through those things in your mind's eye.' It might have been Walters's crisp report writing that first got him noticed at BP, because in his early days in the company juniors used to be called in to take the minutes of the management meetings.

He went straight from National Service into BP, in October 1954. He had decided that he wanted to be involved in a company that was large, significant and international. BP plunged the young ex-officer into a general office, as one of sixty clerks. No one had the slightest idea how to make use of his graduate abilities and he did a very humble, what he called 'Cratchiteer's' job, after Bob Cratchit, the clerk in Dickens's *A Christmas Carol*. 'We'd talk about Cratchiting away all day at our little hand-operated calculating machines.' Walter laughs. 'Dear, dear. That was all experience, I suppose. I used to look around the general office and think to myself, God, they're so much better at their jobs than I am. They'd flick their calculators over so fast and they all seemed to know what they were doing.'

He had joined, along with three other graduates, at a critical moment in BP's history. Three years earlier the prime minister of Iran, Dr Mussadeq, had nationalized the country's oil industry. BP had begun life as the Anglo-Persian Oil Company in 1909, a year after oil was first discovered in the country. By 1951, BP employed 75,000 people in Iran, of whom 94% were locals.

BP was forced to stop its Iranian operations when the work permits for its staff were not renewed and no agreement on compensation had been reached on the termination of the concession before it expired. The staff were withdrawn at the beginning of October 1951. In 1954, when Peter Walters was applying for a job, negotiations between Iran, Britain and America were finally reaching a conclusion. He joined the company when it signed the consortium agreement which had been negotiated with the Iranian government. Two months later, the company changed its name from Anglo-Iranian to British Petroleum.

The chairman-to-be was kept firmly in his place. 'After I had been in the company a couple of years, I was in the central supply department, which dealt with planning, shipping, distribution, logistics: getting the right crude oils to the right refineries to optimize output. I remember going to my branch manager one day and saying: "I really don't know what to do with this particular ship because I don't know the cost of Kuwait crude and nobody will tell me." He said: "They won't tell you, Walters, because you're too junior. That is a confidential aspect of the company's business and until you are a branch manager you are not entitled to know." I said: "Well, clearly you're not paying me to be an economist, are you?"' Six months later Walters was given his first promotion.

One of the senior guys, who had been a Lt.-Colonel in the war and came back to a Cratchiteering job, assaulted the head of the typing pool. Not sexually, but he couldn't get some typing done, so he stormed into her office, picked up her typewriter and dumped it into her wastepaper basket. He was sent home and I was made a sub-section head. Six months later I was given a proper promotion and made a section head and a year after that, namely after four years, I was made an assistant to the manager. And after five years, I was sent to New York.

BP had formed a joint company with Sinclair Oil, an American company that has since disappeared. One objective was to sell BP's abundant Kuwait crude oil to the east coast of America, using the extensive Sinclair pipeline system to move the oil into the US interior.

A few months after Walters and his wife arrived in New York the American government imposed oil import controls. He almost had a non-job, but the deal with Sinclair still made BP a couple of million dollars a year. Walters used his time well, exploring the US oil industry. 'I used to go down to Texas and talk to people. I had to try and sell Kuwait crude in Texas and I remember going to one small refiner who was on a Sinclair pipeline, and he said: "Who the hell's BP anyway?" I said: "It's a little company that produces more oil than Texas."'

Walters was recalled to London after two years to take over BP's Tokyo office for four years. The week he returned, a colleague in the same general supply and distribution area died, while another executive in the same area became the first BP employee to desert to one of the new American oil companies in London. Walters was told to find some temporary lodgings and help out. After six months he asked humbly: 'Excuse me, sir, I really do wonder if I'm going to Tokyo, because if not my wife and I think we ought to buy a house.' 'Good God!' came the reply, 'are you still in a bedsit in Chelsea? Didn't they tell you, we've given Tokyo to someone else.' That about summed up BP's career planning and communications at the time, Walters says. It built up an impression in him of how not to do it, which he hopes he has recently helped change. But he feels it did him no harm.

The next four years were very significant, particularly because BP was then just starting, ahead of other oil companies, to computerize its supplies and refining operations. As an economist, Walters was involved in analysing the factors and resources involved in this operation in his capacity as manager of the main supply department, a job he had acquired because the man trying to do it before him had had a nervous breakdown. Walters's luck looked as though it was running strongly and he was beginning to be noticed as a young man who could cope with new challenges and get things done.

About two years later his divisional boss called him in and said: 'Walters, how would you like to go to New York again?' Although Walters did not realize it at the time, this was as near to the big break as makes no difference. Once again the work turned out to be less than onerous, but the position – his title was Commercial Vice President – turned out to be very privileged:

> There was plenty of time to meet other oil companies and find out what was going on. And I saw all the board papers and notes from London, which were sent officially to New York so we would know what was going on. That was almost the first time I knew what was happening in those areas of the company other than my own. The chairman of the day, Neville Gass or Maurice Bridgeman, or the managing directors, would come out to New York and say: 'Walters, I'm going over to see the chairman of Esso or the senior vice-president, you'd better take me and sit in on the meeting.' That was fascinating, meeting the great men of the day.

It was a two-way acquaintance. The great men of the oil industry began to know Peter Walters and he was firmly marked as a coming man at BP.

He returned to London after two and a half years in May 1967, just in time for the Six-Day War in the Middle East. Walters had been destined to go to central planning, but instead he was put in charge of operations as assistant general manager. 'They needed someone who could look after all the ships and the chartering. There was a deputy chairman, Brian Dummett, in charge of a daily War Council in the boardroom, which I attended. That was a testing time.'

Under the command of Major General Mordechai Hod, the Israeli air force launched its pre-emptive strike against Egypt's air force on the morning of Monday, 5 June 1967. At the end of the Six-Day War, the West Bank of the Jordan, the Golan Heights and the whole of Sinai were under the control of Israel's armed forces, which commanded the whole length of the Suez Canal. It was the end of the beginning. Three weeks later the Egyptians set an ambush ten miles south of Port

Said and the first shots in what became known as the War of Attrition were fired. The Suez Canal was blocked indefinitely and BP had to bring its oil to the West the long way round Africa.

Peter Walters was mowing the lawn of his home in Highgate at eleven o'clock one Saturday shortly afterwards when the telephone rang. BP's head of chartering wanted to speak to him urgently. 'We've just had Aristotle Onassis on the phone,' he said. 'He wants to know whether we want to charter his oil tankers.'

'All of them?' Walters asked incredulously. Onassis owned approximately two and a half million tons deadweight of tankers, the biggest independent fleet in the world.

'Yes. He's collected them all together and it's an all-or-nothing deal for one year. He is giving us a first option until noon today.'

'Can't you stall him until Monday?' Walters asked.

'No. He says we have to decide today.'

'I'll ring you back,' Walters said.

He thought furiously. He knew he would be unlikely to find any members of the board willing to take an instant decision, assuming they were available. Onassis's asking price was high, but the only way BP was going to be able to transport its Middle Eastern crude to Europe was going to be via the Cape. And even if it did not need all Onassis's ships, it could sub-charter them.

He rang his chartering manager back at ten to twelve and told him to take them.

Sunday was a difficult day. But by Monday tanker charter rates were already shading higher and a week later they had doubled. The rewards were not long in coming. Walters was made general manager of the department then in 1971 there was a major reorganization of BP that created four regional directors, one layer below the board. Walters was made regional director of the western hemisphere.

Then towards the end of 1972, just as I was about to go off on a flight to Canada, I had a message to call at the chairman's house in Kensington. He told me: 'Walters,' – I'm not sure he knew what my first name was then – 'Walters, there's a BP main board meeting next Thursday. You're going to be away, so I thought I ought to tell you that I'm proposing to make you a managing director when Billy [Lord Strathalmond] retires.' I nearly fell off the chair. I really didn't expect that. I was forty-one.

He was surprised when it came, but it was an achievement he had always aspired to. He admits the climb to the top had been a strain. He had been with the company for eighteen years and had had twelve different jobs in that time. He and his wife had also reared three young children.

> When they got chicken pox and mumps, I got chicken pox and mumps, you know. My poor wife. I'd quite often leave her when I had to go off abroad somewhere. There were real strains on the nuclear family. Neither she nor I were Londoners, but here we were living in London, with no family support. A lot of people do not stand the pace. Within the selection process, which includes luck and ability, there is survival as well – physical and mental resilience. In my career there were several accidents along the way to people who might otherwise have had my opportunities. They were all capable, well regarded people.

During the 1970s, BP was hit by two great oil price shocks – in 1973, when OPEC first decided to set its own prices, and in 1979. In the same decade BP lost access to most of its supplies of OPEC oil. Its Libyan assets were nationalized by Colonel Gaddafy in 1971. Nigeria followed suit in 1979 and the ayatollahs struck their blow against Western imperialism soon after that. By 1980, group supplies were down to 149 million tons a year from 234 million tons in 1972.

There were compensating successes. BP was stimulated into developing the North Sea as fast as possible, bringing the Forties field into operation in 1975, to produce the first oil to be pumped ashore from the British sector. This was financed by the largest wholly private bank advance – £370m – ever yet arranged. Thanks to inflation, this huge investment has since paled compared to the cost of developing the Magnus field, which at £1.3 billion became BP's biggest ever offshore investment. In addition, there was the even more daunting development of the Kuparuk oilfield in Alaska, which is a story in itself.

However, as BP's potted history, *The Road from Persia*, explains:

> It seems probable that the late 1970s will come to be seen as a watershed in the company's development. These were the years when the traditional, integrated oil company gave way to a diversified business with a wider spread of geographical interests ... The foundations were laid for a reshaped BP in which coal, minerals, gas,

nutrition, detergents, computer systems and telecommunications would all come to take their place alongside the existing oil and petrochemicals activities.

Already some of these diversifications are under scrutiny by Peter Walters. After all, he was selected because he was the man most likely to put BP under the microscope of profit first, last and above everything else.

There has always been a perpetual question of succession at BP, as in any large organization. It would be exceptional if there were not a great deal of manoeuvring at the top. Speculation reached fever pitch during Walters's predecessor's tenure of office. Did Sir David Steel plan the rivalry between Walters and Christopher Laidlaw, when he made them both deputy chairmen on the same day? He took the highly unusual step of issuing a memorandum to the staff announcing that a decision on who should succeed him would not be taken until later. It prompted press comment and a whirlwind of gossip in the corridors of the powerless. As Walters said:

> When the choice was made, Laidlaw was fifty-nine and I was ten years younger. The tradition had been that the BP chairman went on until sixty-five. The two previous chairmen, David Steel and Eric Drake, had both been fifty-nine when they were appointed, so Laidlaw believed himself in no way too old. He probably thought that as I would still be only fifty-five six years hence, there was plenty of time for me to be chairman after him. I don't know, frankly, how the board made their decision.

But he knew he deserved his promotion. There is no false modesty about Walters. 'I suppose I was the most employable pinch-hitter they'd got. They thought I could handle almost anything. And I suppose I had proved it.'

Peter Walters is not a revolutionary, imposing radical changes on a resisting BP. On the contrary, he is an outstanding example of a system choosing the right man from within its ranks to do the job that was needed. Walters has not created a new management structure. That was already in place. The current BP management organization was announced at the end of 1980 and was the result of three years' thought by the group's Organization Planning Committee, of which Walters was a member. The new BP organization differentiated between group head office, the operating businesses and BP's supporting services. It also introduced what it called a management 'matrix', which was designed to make managers, especially of BP's part-owned associate companies around the world, act in the group's overall interest as well as for local advantage. The theory was that this would help push responsibility away from the centre. Peter Walters's great achievement has been in putting this theory into practice.

What has happened to the oil industry in the last thirteen years has been so incredible that it is impossible to forecast what will happen in the next five. How BP survives, however, is vital to the whole of the UK. Peter Walters, it might be argued, is the most important of all Britain's top businessmen. Thank goodness he is so clearly the right man for the job.

The Rewards

If there is a prayer for the New Elite, it might be the one for generosity by Ignatius Loyola:

> To give and not to count the cost;
> To fight and not to heed the wounds;
> To toil and not to seek for rest;
> To labour and not to ask for any reward save that of knowing that we do Thy will.

As patron saint of chief executives, Loyola is an apt choice. He was, after all, the founder of the Jesuits, that disciplined society whose bold enterprises beyond the seas enabled Catholicism to repair in some measure the losses it had incurred in Europe. However, the comparison cannot be taken too far. Loyola may have been happy to have received his reward in heaven, but the New Elite are not averse to enjoying some of their rewards now.

Indeed, they believe they ought to be handsomely rewarded for their services in order to set an example to the rest of us that industry, in both senses of the word, is worthwhile. John Egan says quite bluntly that chief executives of major companies ought to be paid so highly that they become the wealthiest people in the land, purely in order to attract the best talent into creating wealth for the whole country.

David Plastow is of a like mind. He admits to feeling slightly abashed at the fortune he earned last year, but stresses that this subjective reaction is not one he is going to allow to change his conviction that top managers should be rewarded with top rates of pay.

And Richard Giordano, the highest-paid chief executive of any British company with his mind-boggling pay packet of nearly £17,000 a week, not counting share options and other perquisites, doesn't even pretend to modesty. What he is getting, he says quite bluntly, is what he is worth. Giordano believes, in fact, that executive pay is a reflection of the value of a manager to a company. His view of the relationship between a top manager and the company he works for is not so much that of employer and employee, but more that of a treaty between trading partners. A good executive owes it to his company as much as to himself to put the right value on his services. A valuable package of remuneration is immediate proof that he is a good negotiator, as well as giving him status with his colleagues.

Having said this, however, the variations in the pay of the ten chief executives profiled in *The New Elite* are so wide that it is hard to pretend there is a rate for the job.

	Earnings
Sir Michael Edwardes	£66,808*
(to March 1986)	
Sir John Egan	£172,959
(to December 1985)	
Richard Giordano	£883,100
(to September 1985)	
Sir Stanley Grinstead	£176,289
(to September 1985)	
Sir John Harvey-Jones	£312,991
(to December 1985)	
Sir Christopher Hogg	£126,288
(to March 1986)	
Sir Trevor Holdsworth	£145,000
(to December 1985)	
Colin Marshall	£100,900
(to March 1986)	
Sir David Plastow	£211,006
(to December 1985)	
Sir Peter Walters	£260,972
(to December 1985)	

* only executive chairman for part of year

The mean salary works out at around £200,000 a year, which is about £5,000 a week and roughly twenty-five times the average industrial wage. By US and European standards it is not high, but nobody can pretend the New Elite are exactly starving. When the perquisites of office like free cars, chauffeurs, health insurance, travel, meals and incidental expenses are added in, all of them are extremely well off. They are also nicely cushioned against the future by handsome pension contributions and that most fashionable of executive rewards, the share option scheme.

Share options are how top businessmen are scoring these days. The popularity of share options is another product of Tory reform of the tax system, largely displacing exaggerated pension payments as the method of giving successful employees what amounts to a tax-free bonus. They have the attraction of relating how much top management gets to how well it does for the company's shareholders. It has to be admitted that as a method of reward the giving of share options is a fairly blunt instrument. Share prices rise and fall for a number of reasons that have little to do with pure trading performance. However, most of the New Elite think that share options are a fair yardstick, as they believe their ultimate responsibility is to their companies' shareholders.

	Shares	Options
Sir Michael Edwardes (to March 1986)	175,750	None
Sir John Egan (to December 1985)	12,000	245,812
Richard Giordano (to September 1985)	65,128	400,000
Sir Stanley Grinstead (to September 1985)	245,936*	224,184
Sir John Harvey-Jones (to December 1985)	6,367	20,000**
Sir Christopher Hogg (to March 1986)	35,000	256,788
Sir Trevor Holdsworth (to December 1985)	1,000	196,691
Colin Marshall (to March 1986)	N/A	N/A
Sir David Plastow (to December 1985)	5,375	213,245
Sir Peter Walters (to December 1985)	8,582	88,652

* including 140,400 non-beneficial
** 55,000 options already exercised
(Statistics compiled by Monks Partnership, Thaxted.)

Based on share prices in July 1986, the value of the shares and options owned by the New Elite is at least £500,000 a head, with several of them paper millionaires. John Harvey-Jones's shares and options are only worth about £200,000, but he has already cashed in on nearly three times as many options as he retains, so he could have already collected upwards of £500,000. Christopher Hogg and Peter Walters each hold more than £500,000-worth, with Trevor Holdsworth a shade better off at £650,000. Then there is a big jump to David Plastow's rights to about £900,000 worth of Vickers' shares, while over the million mark are John Egan at £1.3m and Richard Giordorno at £1.4m. Stanley Grinstead tops the list at £1.7m, although this includes £500,000 in shares which do not benefit him personally.

It is difficult to calculate exactly how much money the New Elite have made out of buying or being given shares in the companies they run. Executive share options are not free. Senior management is given the opportunity to buy equity at fixed prices, which are usually lower than the then current share price, but not necessarily by much. The advantage is that they can wait until some point in the future when the shares are worth much more due to the success of the company. If the shares do not increase in value, they don't exercise the options and lose nothing. Thanks to a combination of inflation, a booming stock market and their own efforts, however, there is no doubt that most of the New Elite are sitting on very handsome paper profits.

The odd men out in our list are Michael Edwardes and Colin Marshall. Do not weep too much for them. Marshall collected his fair portion of salary and shares at Hertz and Avis, while Michael Edwardes picked up more than £500,000 in golden handshakes from ICL and Dunlop.

Of course, the stock market is a variable feast. Slump follows boom with the inevitability of the seasons. But then, most of the option holders have time on their side. That said, the New Elite believe implicitly that their remuneration should be directly linked with the success of their companies. They see the money they are paid as a measure of their achievement – almost a reward for virtue. As Dr Johnson wrote: 'There are few ways in which a man can be more innocently employed than in getting money.'

Don't Just Stand There, Do Something!

We can't end without an attempt to arrive at some general conclusions about the stuff the New Elite are made of. It's all very well drawing pretty word pictures of a bunch of high-profile businessmen, but do they collectively add up to a representative sample? Have we, in other words, been portraying the leaders of the pack, or the exceptions who prove the rule?

Judging by that indispensible tool of modern life, the market survey, our top ten are remarkably true to type. By pure coincidence, at the time that we were doing our research, PA Consultants was conducting a Study of Corporate Leadership in Britain, which attracted answers from 256 chief executives of companies in *The Times* Top 1,000.

The average chief executive in Britain, it transpires, is male, aged fifty-two, and married with 2.8 children. Although he is most likely to live in the country within thirty-five minutes of his office, he may also have homes in both the town and the country. He is an inveterate traveller, spending fifty-two nights a year away from home. During his career, he has also experienced working overseas for about three years.

He is an early bird, arriving at the office well before 8.20 am. He is health-conscious, setting time aside for golf, tennis or walking. Jogging is not one of his pleasures – it is too lonely – and more popular pastimes are music, gardening and reading.

He is relatively well-educated. More than half of Britain's chief executives have been to university and a third have been to courses at management or business schools, although only 5% have MBA degrees. Six out of ten attended State schools, 5% did apprenticeships, 4% were trained in the Armed Services and about a quarter are qualified accountants.

A third said that their first management job was a key period in their development as leaders. National Service and overseas postings were formative for many, while others learned from coping with business crises. Crucial lessons in leadership almost all came from moments of intense conflict, such as facing bankruptcy, strikes, redundancies, industrial injuries and takeovers.

Britain's average chief executive professes a high degree of concern for the human factors that make his business competitive and profitable. The PA survey shows an overwhelming preference for a personal approach. Nearly 70% say that people are their most important responsibility, with only 24% putting profit, financial performance and return to shareholders first.

Asked the personal characteristic that they believed had been the most important in their careers, most said it was the ability to communicate. Next came determination and drive, followed by hard work. Other highly valued characteristics are ambition, integrity, leadership, decisiveness, intelligence, compassion and perseverance. And on the subject of leadership, the vast majority said the prime requirement is vision.

It is slightly unnerving to discover how closely our ten equate with the norm. They even share in the general strongly held feelings about the need to educate the next generation of business leaders in the virtues of wealth creation and risk-taking, the need to give young people an industrial upbringing and a climate in which opportunity can flourish. Have we, in our innocence, spent our entire time defining a stereotype?

Up to a point the answer is probably yes. There wouldn't, in fact, be much point to this book if it had been devoted to individuals who are so different from their peer group that their careers offer no lessons for the rest of us. In any case, it is hardly surprising that Britain's top businessmen conform to the average in many respects. After all, they set the standards. Everybody else is probably trying to conform to them. It is equally important to remember that they are career businessmen who have worked their way up through the system over many years.

We would like to think that the New Elite are more open to change than the average businessman, whose natural tendency is to strive for monopoly and stasis. What has brought the New Elite to the fore is the series of exceptional challenges that has faced British industry in the last ten years. What singles out our heroes is that they have been able to cope with changing circumstances in a way that most senior managers demonstrably have not. Whether this is because they are, relatively speaking, lateral thinkers, or because they are simply better at facing hard facts, is arguable. Perhaps the truth is that the New Elite are just tougher and more determined than anyone else. UK industry has become increasingly nasty, brutish and terminal, and there are no signs of a *deus ex machina* saving what is left, unless you count joint ventures with Japanese companies. The New Elite have shown that they can hold the fort.

Don't blame them for doing no more than they promise. That is one of their strengths. Instead, let's hope that their example inspires the rest of British management and, indeed, all of us to try harder and do better.

In the end, that's the secret.

Executive Sayings

Black Economy

'On broad brush issues I think the Tory Government has done very well. I do not accept the need for the present levels of unemployment and I criticize the Government for that. I believe the Black Economy should have been captured. I think the fact that so many people are outside the tax net is a thoroughly unsatisfactory state of affairs. It means the burden on the rest of us is correspondingly higher and, although this may sound a daft thing to say, I believe it erodes the moral fibre of the nation. We used to be a very law-abiding, respectable, honest sort of people.

'I believe the industrial base of this country has been eroded more than was necessary. It is a mistake for the Government to imagine that service industry is going to pay for everything. At the end of the day we can't all end up cutting each others' hair.'

Trevor Holdsworth

Bonus Payments

'I have been committed to executive bonus payments for a long time. This year I will earn a great deal of money and I must admit I am a little uncomfortable about the amount, but I think the principle is very healthy indeed. Vickers needs to pay European and world level salaries to remain competitive and the bonuses are an incentive to the boys who are driving to get to the top.

'I think you have to have purely mechanistic systems – no judgmental element at all. For our board, including me, it is based on earnings per share smoothed over three years. It's a known part of my agreement with the company – and it's eyeable for anyone who wants to see it.'

David Plastow

Capitalism

'In practice the alternatives that were thought to cure the ills of capitalism have all failed. Now we are coming to a new period when the virtues of capitalism are beginning to be realized. The manager in private industry will be operating against a much more sympathetic background in the long run. It is a question of getting compassionate capitalism. Once you have that, you really have got a very good system.'

Trevor Holdsworth

Commitment

'If people think you care, think you are emotionally committed to them, they will go to great lengths, even extremes, to get done what is necessary. And of course people judge this quite intuitively. None of the pretty speeches about concern for colleagues or for customers means anything. What counts is action: a series of acts that cause those working with and for you to believe that you are, first and foremost, concerned about them and their needs.

'I am not suggesting that good leaders are necessarily nice, understanding human beings. Some of the best I have known have been harsh, truculent, difficult people – but they are committed. They meant and delivered what they said. They cared. They were willing to donate more than they asked of anyone else. Above all, even when they were asking for more than they were getting, they made it clear that the concerns of those led were a prime consideration.'

Colin Marshall

Competition

'We are in a totally international market. Everywhere we sell our car there is a showroom next door selling something very similar and totally competitive.'

John Egan

'We can't go about our business with one hand tied behind our backs. The maddening characteristic of this country is that it is so insular. It will not look outside and take its standards from the rest of the world. It leaves those of us who actually have to match up to overseas competition pretty darned exposed.'

Christopher Hogg

'I am not pessimistic about this country's ability to produce competent people, or high quality goods or ideas. But the other side of the coin is that our competitors are not fools or saints.'

Peter Walters

Customers
'The absolute fundamental aim is to make money out of satisfying customers.'

John Egan

Education
'I submit that much of our business leadership problem in this country stems from our justly famous educational system. It turns out superbly trained analytical minds that see all the intellectual elements of any business problem, but simply lack the impetus to do anything about them ... In other words, our university system supplies us with extremely quick-thinking analytical minds that have comparatively little understanding or empathy with the needs of other people.'

Colin Marshall

'I qualify the statement that the best people don't go into industry – of course, it is true that they don't – by saying that they would not necessarily be God's gift to it if they did. Your chap from Eton and Trinity, Cambridge with a first in this and that has a whole lot of values that aren't going to be too helpful. Industry needs bright people, sure, but it runs on a great many other people with sterling virtues of other kinds.'

Christopher Hogg

'The truth, unfortunately, is that, for many of our young people, the subjects taught at school are often of little practical value or assistance.

'People may ask why an industrialist should involve himself in educational matters. But the fact is that we in industry are already involved and cannot escape our responsibilities. We are, after all, the people who do much of the recruiting and we must share some of the blame if schools and universities do not understand our requirements.'

Peter Walters

Ethics

'It horrifies me to hear that ethics is only an optional extra at Harvard Business School.'

John Harvey-Jones

Exchange Rates

'I think British industry spends too much bloody time talking about exchange rates. If you appreciate the scale at which money flows these days – the turnover in the world money markets every twenty-four hours is in excess of the total monetary reserves of the Western World – you realize the scale of the problem.

'To say to the Government, "Fix the exchange rate," is bloody daft. Margaret Thatcher was wrong in 1980/81 when the rate against the dollar was 2.40, because she did have scope to lower interest rates, but to say, "Let's have a stable exchange rate," is a great speech, but not a practical one.'

David Plastow

Failure

'There is no safe way to be a good leader. You do not win all the time and you have to learn that failure is part of the leadership game, so long as you do not make the same mistake twice.'

Colin Marshall

Fear

'The overriding mood amongst our employees is fear. Most of our employees are well aware that the whole world is in recession. In these circumstances it should be no surprise that the power of management to implement change is at its greatest. However, raw power to act on one side and fear on the other are hardly the basis for a long-lasting productive relationship.'

Richard Giordano

Free Enterprise

'Free enterprise is not just another economic system. Its impact goes beyond our economic lives to some of the basic freedoms that are deeply embedded in our culture. It is acknowledged as the most effective means of allocating resources in society and hence the most likely to create wealth... As businessmen, we have a special responsibility to make the system work and, if it falters, to diagnose with clarity what is wrong and what repairs are necessary.'

Richard Giordano

The Future

'Here is a problem; the models that most of us work from are almost by definition obsolete. Generals usually begin by fighting the last war. I am sadly aware that by the time we have reached the goal I have set in five years' time, I may well have designed an ideal company to cope with conditions five years back.'

John Harvey-Jones

Imports

'Unless we are pragmatic about protecting infant industries, we will not get enough new industrial investment before high quality Far Eastern goods arrive. Why should a manufacturer in a totally new field have to fight immediate import penetration? The key to modular technology is a mass market. In the case of the UK, our own home market, which is the first base on which we could build, is already swamped by imports.'

Peter Walters

Industrial Base

'I think it is demoralized poppycock to say our industrial base cannot be rebuilt. There is nothing beyond us provided we have a world base on which to do it. The problem is that the whole culture of the UK is still not one that puts industrial priorities where it should.'

Christopher Hogg

Industrial Relations

'I do not think there is any magic formula to all this. Just hard work and long hours of talking to everyone, of trying to understand the problems better, of talking about and testing solutions with everyone concerned.'

Colin Marshall

Leadership

'What is the essential element any successful leader absolutely must have? I think it can be reduced to one word and a rather simple one at that: caring.

'I cannot claim that caring leadership is terribly clever or even terribly new. I can only promise that within my experience it works better than anything else.'

Colin Marshall

'There have always been natural leaders and natural managers who have been able ... to get extraordinary results out of ordinary people.'

John Harvey-Jones

Living Standards

'The only way we can preserve our living standards, our values and the social choices we care so desperately about as a nation is through industrial success ... We are only going to succeed in this country when we realize the value of the manager to our complex social world and when he, or she, is seen as a vital and key ingredient for success nationally, as well as in the enterprises in which we work.'

John Harvey-Jones

Management

'I believe passionately that management is an art ... Because management is an art, there are no limits to its development, no limits as to how far one can develop oneself and no limits to individuality and originality in our practice of it.'

John Harvey-Jones

'If we are to break out of a vicious circle of despair and failure, management must take the lead.'

John Egan

'I think there is a shortage of quality managers in this country. Why is this so? One reason is that business has not been seen as the most attractive career, so the quality input has not been as high as it should.

'Secondly, you've had a couple of decades of failure. This failure has demoralized people and has given them the wrong kind of training.

'Let's divide it up: one third failure, one third government, one third unions. If you look back to 1979, just before Mrs Thatcher came into power, you had exchange controls, price controls, wage controls. What did a manager do when he came into his office in the morning? You've gotta wonder! What they did was they retired to teach, tend the roses.

173

'Could any of this have changed without Mrs Thatcher? The whole atmosphere has changed. For all her faults, she may be the person who brought us back from the abyss.'

Richard Giordano

Oil

'If we had set up a trust fund for the nation, as it were, and put half the government's oil revenues into the fund, we could have the most incredible situation in the UK in the year 2000. But we ain't done that. What I don't know is whether in practice most of the oil money has been invested abroad in any case. I'm a bit doubtful about that.'

Michael Edwardes

Pay

'British managers were paid nothing. In the 1970s you had people behaving like capitalists but living like paupers. You couldn't pay them more because tax rates were so high they didn't keep it. A good hot dinner was worth more than £1,000 a year. No wonder that people fiddled their expenses.

'I remember when I was running companies in Europe, the Brit was cheap. I could hire someone from this country for half the price of a German or a Frenchman, and he was usually massively overqualified as well. The man was pathetically pleased to be paid anything.'

'If we want good international companies, we simply have to pay people to run them...'

'Why should it be that everyone is very pleased that Steve Davis is a millionaire when all he does is play snooker? Admittedly he plays it extremely well. If somebody creates a fine company, though, that exports hundreds of millions of pounds' worth of goods and adds lustre to Britain's international reputation, and also makes the country as well as the company wealthy, it seems to be anathema to the British if he is rewarded highly.'

John Egan

Politicians

'I think it is incredible that politicians pontificate on companies when they have so little idea of what they need. For example, I was intrigued by the Labour spokesman for industry saying Jaguar needs cash. We don't need cash! We need managerial capabilities and a technological base, which we've got to create and organize ourselves. There is simply no other way of doing it.'

John Egan

Price Controls

'One of the big reasons, in my judgment, for the unemployment and trauma over the past few years was the Prices and Incomes Policy, under which we operated in the 1970s. All you had to do at that time was to prove that your costs had gone up by 10% or whatever in the last quarter and you were allowed to put up your prices by the same percentage.

'It took a generation of managers' eyes off the ball. They forgot about the marketplace. Good management would have been aware of the need to be efficient, to take out redundant plant and so on, but all that was dammed up. When the scales were finally torn away from their eyes, they had years of neglecting their manufacturing base to remedy.'

Stanley Grinstead

Privatization

'The reasons for privatization are still clear. The benefit of privatizing is that you remove services from the daily push and pull of politics. However, you do need to recognize that corporations like British Gas are monopolies, and they need to be recognized as such. They are going to misbehave if they can, and we will pay for it if they are not properly controlled.'

Richard Giordano

Protection

'I can write you a prescription for a greater degree of optimism, but it would need, I think, a breathing space during which industry is protected. I think it is quite wrong, for example, that Spain, on entering the Common Market, can impose a 21% tariff on imports of cars from Britain, but can export modular, world-scale Ford Fiestas to the UK paying only 3% duty. That is an example of a modular technology upsetting the supposition that Germany or Britain has a ten-year competitive development advantage.'

Peter Walters

Research and Development
'We are easily capable of keeping up with our foreign competitors, providing we spend enough. If you don't spend on research and development and on new equipment, you don't have the technology base.'

John Egan

Responsibility
'I believe most of us in the private sector are motivated – I certainly am – by a deep feeling of responsibility for the people in our organization.'

John Harvey-Jones

Return on Capital
'Return on capital is the way we drive the guys. It's the thing that leads through most directly to our earnings per share, which is what really matters. It is fundamental to driving the business, because it is related to our ability to pay dividends. The simple arithmetic we apply to, say, a factory in Woking or Edinburgh is return on capital. Everyone understands that. It forces a proper estimation of prices and a constant attack on costs.'

David Plastow

Success
'Most successes come from ignoring the obvious.'

Trevor Holdsworth

Taxation
'The Thatcher Government brought some fundamental changes that I don't believe a lot of commentators have actually recognized. One of the most fundamental was reducing the top rate of tax to 60%.

'The 60% limit meant that for the first time someone running a large public company could take home more than someone running a builder's yard.'

John Egan

Technology
'Technology is moving so fast that in most industries there is a chance of getting back into the game again. This country has many advantages and our people have great innate abilities. History tells us that no

company is invincible. Just when it seems strongest, it is most vulnerable. I'm an optimist about what can be done on the business front.'

Christopher Hogg

'I believe that technology these days is so modular that the idea that Western countries had a five- or ten-year lead is no longer true. The modular technology has totally obliterated our learning advantage. New competitors can be on our doorstep and penetrating our markets before we have had a breathing space to revitalize our own production.'

Peter Walters

Trade
'The biggest threat we face is that the US might introduce trade restraint.'

David Plastow

Trades Unions
'Disciplining the trades unions was absolutely fundamental. When I took over at Jaguar, the idea that we could run the company for a year and not have a single strike was not feasible. People would have thought I was in cloud-cuckoo land.

'I believe the unions had little good intent and no good ideas. They were constantly grabbing for more and more for doing less and less. At a time when their productivity was already only a third of that in Germany, it seemed a rather pathetic exercise. At the end of it all the last people to believe that Britain was still an immensely wealthy country that could afford to have nobody working at all were the unions.

'By and large the union officials don't seem to have changed their ideas very much. It is almost as though they are imbued with a social model of the world to which we can never measure up. The fact that everyone at Jaguar still has a job and is earning a lot more money and is more contented than before doesn't seem to register.'

John Egan

'Most of us realize that the perversion of the relationship between management and labour is at the root of our productivity problem. We have managed over a long period of time to combine low wages with low productivity to produce much higher unit costs than almost all of our competitors in world trade. No doubt there are many villains in this piece ...'

Richard Giordano

Thatcher

'Margaret Thatcher did not give managers the power to manage. The revolution in management, I believe, was actually brought about before she came in. She gave it impetus by the economic policies that followed. The trouble is that a great deal of our industrial base went out with the bathwater.'

Michael Edwardes

Training

'I do not believe our universities, our graduate schools or many of our businesses themselves are training leaders. We have been too concerned with form, with concepts such as marketing, strategic management or productivity – important as they may be – to persuade young people moving into business to understand that effective leadership comes from dealing effectively with other people.'

Colin Marshall

'I believe that management training is best done by experiential means rather than from case histories and books. Confucius he say: read and forget, see and remember, do and understand.'

John Harvey-Jones

The Truth

'Always tell the truth. It is usually rather effective!'

Colin Marshall

Unemployment

'It's all very well calling for Government action on this or that. I think most of the things the Tories have done have been right in terms of Vickers's experience. More compassion about unemployment would be a good speech, but there is no simple solution to this. If the Labour Party returns to power, it will find the total industrial structure has changed.'

David Plastow

Values

'I am bound to say that I am a strong believer in the necessity to seek for congruence between the values of the company and the values of the manager. You cannot in industry work totally on the principle that the end justifies the means. The ends have to be felt to be good. People want to take pride in themselves and their work, and they need to have faith that the end product, wealth creation, is a decent and honourable and essential social task.'

John Harvey-Jones

Work

'I don't think working for a living has ever been highly regarded in this country. We have always preferred to inherit money or to have some strange knack like playing snooker. Even the Great Train Robbers got a grudging respect. To say that you have earned large sums of money has always brought a great deal of criticism.'

John Egan